PARTY CROCHET

PARTY CROCHET

SUE WHITING

First published in North America in 2007 by

CRE**A**TIVE
HOMEOWNER®

Upper Saddle River, NJ
Creative Homeowner® is a registered trademark of Federal
Marketing Corporation

Current printing (last digit): 10 9 8 7 6 5 4 3 2 1
Library of Congress card number: 2006929062
ISBN-10: 1-58011-330-3
ISBN-13: 978-1-58011-330-4

Senior editor: Corinne Masciocchi
Pattern checker: Sue Horan
Artworks: Ben Cracknell, Carrie Hill and Kuo Kang Chen
Photographer: Sian Irvine
Designer: Isobel Gillan
Production: Hazel Kirkman
Editorial direction: Rosemary Wilkinson

Reproduction by Pica Digital PTE Ltd, Singapore
Printed and bound by Times Offset, Malaysia

CREATIVE HOMEOWNER
A division of Federal Marketing Corp.
24 Park Way
Upper Saddle River, NJ 07458
www.creativehomeowner.com

Publisher's note

Some of the original designs in *Party
Crochet* were done with Goldfingering,
which is not widely available in the United
States. However, Lion Glitterspun, Rowan
Lurex, and DMC thread can be subsituted
for Goldfingering. Substitutions have been
made where appropriate.

Contents

Introduction

Luscious Lurex®, mouth-watering mohair, cuddly chenille, romantic ribbons and sparkling specialty yarns are easily transformed into perfect party wear with a little help from a crochet hook!

Crochet is easy – take a ball of yarn, a crochet hook and a little inspiration and you are ready to go. And here you should find more than enough inspiration to help you create that perfect party outfit – with surprisingly little effort. Whether you are looking for glamorous and elegant evening wear or a funky little number to pop on with jeans and a T-shirt to visit friends, there's something here for everyone. It doesn't matter if you are a total novice crocheter or not, that shouldn't stop you – there are just as many quick and easy projects here as there are ones that might challenge you!

Crochet is growing in popularity – both as a craft and as a fashion statement. Nearly every big name now includes a little crochet somewhere in their collection – from main street stores to the biggest couture houses. And now you can be up there, too. Once you've got the knack of a few basic stitches, you are ready to start to create your very own "designer original."

Almost all the hand knitting yarns that are available now in yarn stores can be used for crochet. Here we'll take some of the best and most exciting yarns and turn them into stunning garments you'll love to wear.

With crochet, there's only one stitch on your hook at any time so there's very little chance of dropping stitches and making mistakes. All the different crochet stitches are based on one simple principle – insert the hook into the work, wrap the yarn over the hook and pull a loop through. That's all there is to it! It's just the *way* the hook is inserted and how the yarn is wrapped over that creates the stunning effects so easy to achieve in crochet. And here you'll find all the techniques you need to help you on your way as well as the patterns you'll need to create your very own masterpiece.

And why not try adding beads and sequins to your crochet to add even more impact? Here there are lots of designs to make that use them to great effect, whether you want to just add a few beads to try a new technique or masses of sequins to make a dramatic statement. And the selection of beads and sequins available is vast, too – from subtle seed beads to glamorous crystals, from pearls to paillette sequins. So long as you can thread it onto your yarn, you can use it!

Crochet is fun – so it's the ideal way to make fun party wear. So what's stopping you? Start flipping through now, choose your design and get the party started!

Basic Information

WHAT YOU WILL NEED

All that is really needed to crochet an item is a crochet hook, some yarn and a pattern.

Crochet hooks

Crochet hooks, like knitting needles, come in lots of different sizes and are often made of different materials. Larger hooks are usually plastic, but it is possible to buy hooks made from bamboo – many people find this type particularly easy and comfortable to work with. Smaller hooks are usually metal, although some may consist of a metal hook and shank encased in a plastic handle.

The size of the hook used determines the size of the stitches being made, which is also usually governed by the thickness of the yarn. Thick yarns are usually worked using a chunky hook, while fine yarns generally require a small hook.

Nowadays crochet hook sizes are generally given in a metric size – but if you have old hooks, carrying an older imperial measurement, you need to know what the metric equivalent is.

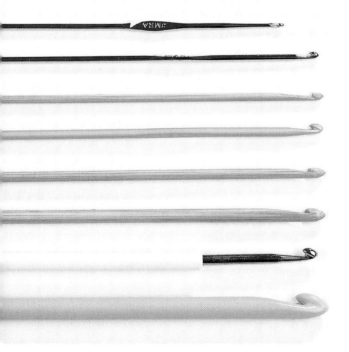
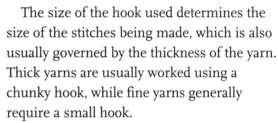

Crochet hook conversion chart

Metric	Old UK	USA
2.00 mm	14	B / 1
2.25 mm	13	B / 1
2.50 mm	12	C / 2
3.00 mm	11	D / 3
3.25 mm	10	D / 3
3.50 mm	9	E / 4
3.75 mm	–	F / 5
4.00 mm	8	G / 6
4.50 mm	7	7
5.00 mm	6	H / 8
5.50 mm	5	I / 9
6.00 mm	4	J / 10
6.50 mm	3	K / 10¹/₂
7.00 mm	2	–
8.00 mm	0	L / 11
9.00 mm	00	M / 13
10.00 mm	000	N / 15

When making the slip knot, ensure that the end of
the yarn that tightens the loop is the cut end of the
yarn, not the end leading to the ball – this will allow
the slip knot to be pulled up tighter later to neaten
the work.

When working any crochet stitch, the yarn should
always be wrapped over the hook in the same way –
over, round and under.

Yarns

Almost any yarn sold for hand knitting can
be used for crochet – but some are easier to
use than others! Beginners will find smooth
yarns far easier to work with than textured
ones. A fancy yarn that has a fluffy or boucle
surface can easily catch on the crochet hook,
making it difficult to pull the yarn through
when working the stitches, and tricky to find
exactly where to insert the hook.

The yarns used in this book are varied –
some are fine smooth yarns, either plain or
sparkly, and some are heavily textured – but all
are ideally suited to making stylish party wear.

- **Colinette Giotto** 50% cotton, 40% rayon,
  10% nylon, $157^1/_2$ yds/144 m per $3^1/_2$ oz
  (100 g) hank.
- **Lion Brand Incredible** 100% nylon, 110 yds
  /100 m per $1^3/_4$ oz (50 g) ball.
- **Rowan Cotton Glace** 100% cotton, 137 yds
  /115 m per $1^3/_4$ oz (50 g) ball.
- **Rowan Kidsilk Haze** 70% super kid mohair,
  30% silk, 229 yds/210 m per 1 oz (25 g) ball.
- **Rowan Kidsilk Night** 67% super kid mohair,
  18% silk, 10% polyester, 5% nylon, 227
  yds/208 m per 1 oz (25 g) ball.
- **Rowan Lurex® Shimmer** 80% viscose, 20%
  polyester, 104 yds/95 m per 1 oz (25 g) ball.
- **Rowan RYC Soft Lux** 64% extra fine merino
  wool, 10% angora, 24% nylon, 2% metallic
  fiber, 137 yds/125 m per $1^3/_4$ oz (50 g) ball.
- **Sirdar Frenzy** 66% polyester, 34% nylon,
  47 yds/43 m per $1^3/_4$ oz (50 g) ball.

- **Sirdar Wow!** 100% polyester, $63^1/_2$ yds/58 m
  per $3^1/_2$ oz (100 g) ball.
- **Twilleys Goldfingering** 80% viscose,
  20% metallized polyester, 219 yds/200 m
  per $1^3/_4$ oz (50 g) ball.
- **Twilleys Silky** 100% viscose, 219 yds/200 m
  per $1^3/_4$ oz (50 g) ball.
- **Wendy Chic** 60% nylon, 30% polyester,
  10% metallized polyester, $87^1/_2$ yds/80 m
  per $1^3/_4$ oz (50 g) ball.

Extras

Only a few extra items are needed to complete
a crochet pattern. Scissors are needed to cut
the yarn, and a tape measure is required to
check the gauge and that the work is the
correct length. A blunt-tipped sewing needle –
like the sort used for cross-stitch or tapestry –
is needed to sew up the pieces. Everything else
that may be required – such as beads or
buttons – will be detailed with the pattern
instructions.

THE IMPORTANCE OF GAUGE

Gauge refers to the number of stitches or
rows per in / cm. If many hours are to be
spent making a crochet item, it's a good idea
to make sure it's going to be the correct size!
It is vitally important to the success of a
project that the gauge achieved matches that
stated in the pattern, as the gauge governs the
final size of the crocheted pieces. If the gauge
is not correct, not only will the pieces not fit

together as they should, but the finished item will not be the correct size. It may also mean that extra yarn will be required, or some may be left over.

Checking the gauge

Before beginning the actual item, a gauge swatch should be worked. Crochet has a tendency to pull in slightly as the work grows, so this gauge swatch must be quite large – ideally 6 in (15 cm) square. Work this gauge swatch in the stitch pattern given in the "Gauge" section using the hook size stated and the correct yarn. Once the swatch is complete, lay it flat and mark out 4 in (10 cm) both across and along the rows with pins.

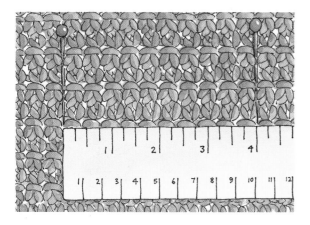

Count the number of stitches and rows (or pattern repeats if this is how the gauge is given) between these marked points and check that it matches the gauge stated on the pattern. If there are more stitches or rows than stated in the pattern, the work is too tight and another swatch should be worked using a larger size hook. If there are too *few* stitches or rows, the work is too loose and a smaller size hook will be needed. Once the correct gauge has been obtained, use the size hook that achieved this gauge for the item.

THE BASIC STITCHES

Crochet is very simple as it basically consists of just a few different stitches, all of which are worked in a very similar way. It is their heights that vary. There is only one stitch on the hook at any one time and the new stitches are worked by inserting the hook through the work, wrapping the yarn over the hook and pulling these loops of yarn through the stitch already on the hook.

Slip knot

To start the work, there needs to be the first original stitch on the hook. It is formed by making a slip knot and slipping it over the hook.

Make the slip knot by forming the cut end into a loop. Insert the hook through this loop and pull another loop of yarn through the first loop. Gently pull on the cut end to tighten this second loop around the body of the hook and the first stitch is created.

Chain stitch

This is the basic starting point for almost all crochet projects.

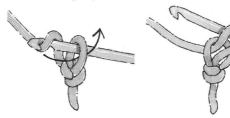

To make a chain stitch, wrap the yarn over the hook by passing it over, round and under the hook. Now gently ease this new loop of yarn through the loop on the hook to complete the chain stitch.

Slip stitch

A slip stitch adds virtually no extra height to the work and is often used to join stitches together.

To work a slip stitch, insert the hook into the work as detailed in the pattern and take the yarn over the hook in the same way as for a chain stitch. Now bring this new loop of yarn through both the work and the stitch on the hook.

Single crochet

One of the most basic and frequently used crochet stitches, a single crochet is a short, neat stitch.

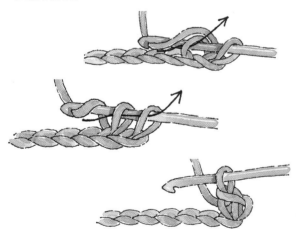

Start the single crochet stitch by inserting the hook into the work, taking the yarn over the hook and pulling this new loop of yarn through the work – there are now 2 loops of yarn on the hook. Take the yarn over the hook again and bring this new loop of yarn through both of the loops on the hook to complete the stitch.

Double crochet

Another commonly used stitch is the double crochet stitch – quite a tall, upright stitch.

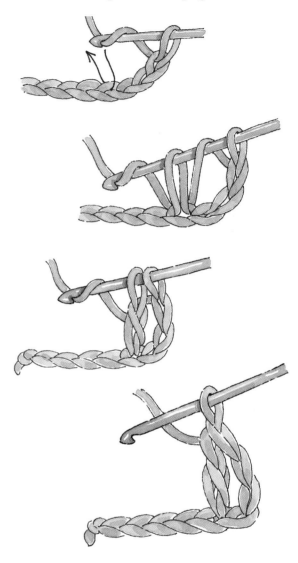

Make a double crochet by wrapping the yarn over the hook before inserting it into the work. Insert the hook into the work and wrap the yarn over the hook again. Bring this loop of yarn through the work so that there are 3 loops of yarn on the hook. Wrap the yarn over the hook and pull this new loop through just 2 of the loops on the hook – there are now 2 loops on the hook. Again, wrap the yarn over the hook and pull this loop through both of the loops already on the hook to finish the stitch.

Double crochet variations

A double crochet stitch is created by wrapping the yarn over the hook once before inserting it into the work. Taller double crochet-like stitches can be created by wrapping the yarn over the hook more times before it is inserted into the work.

To make a **treble**, wrap the yarn over the hook twice before inserting it into the work. Now wrap the yarn over the hook again and draw this new loop through the work, leaving 4 loops on the yarn. Wrap the yarn over the hook once more and pull this loop through 2 of the 4 loops on the hook – 3 loops are now on the hook. Continue wrapping the yarn over the hook and bringing this new loop through pairs of loops already on the hook until there is just one loop left on the hook. For a treble, this is done a total of 3 times.

To make a **double treble** stitch, wrap the yarn over the hook 3 times before inserting it and repeat the (yarn over hook and draw new loop through 2 existing loops) process a total of 4 times. Similarly, to make a **triple treble**, wrap the yarn over the hook 4 times before it is inserted into the work and repeat the (yarn over hook and draw new loop through 2 existing loops) process a total of 5 times.

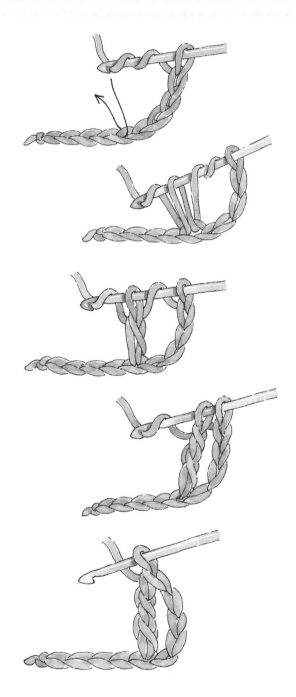

■ It's a good idea to collect everything you need for your item before you begin so that it is at hand while working.

■ It is essential to check your crochet gauge for every item made. While you may achieve the gauge stated with the hook stated on a dense crochet fabric, if the design uses a lot of lacy or chain stitches, you may need to adjust your hook size. Many crocheters work dense stitch-patterns and chains at a different gauge to those incorporating lots of chain lengths.

■ Make sure you read through the explanation of any special abbreviations before starting to work so that you fully understand how to construct this special stitch, or stitch group.

■ Many crocheters find it easier to follow a pattern by circling the figures that relate to the size they are making before starting. To avoid permanently marking the pattern, circle these figures in pencil so that these markings can be erased later.

Half double crochet

This stitch is a combination of a single crochet and a double crochet stitch and is about halfway between the two in height.

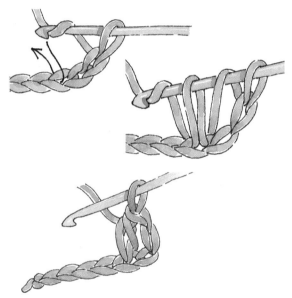

Start the half double crochet in the same way you would a double crochet – wrap the yarn over the hook and insert the hook into the work. Take the yarn over the hook and draw this new loop through the work so that there are 3 loops on the hook. Now complete the half double crochet as though it were a single crochet stitch by wrapping the yarn over the hook again and drawing this new loop through **all** the loops on the hook.

PLACING THE STITCHES

Varying effects can be created with the same basic crochet stitch by inserting the hook through the work in different ways.

Through the top of a stitch

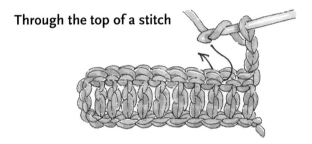

This is the most common placement for the new stitch and is the way the hook should be inserted into the work unless the pattern states otherwise. Across the top of stitches there will nearly always be a "V" shape formed by 2 strands of yarn. Insert the hook through the work, from front to back, under both of these strands to make the new stitch.

Through one loop only

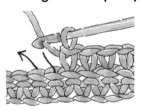 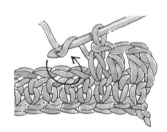

Special effects can be created on the surface of the work by just picking up one of the 2 strands that form the "V" on top of a stitch, when working the new one. Check the pattern to see which of the 2 strands it should be, and insert the hook under this strand only, inserting it from front to back, instead of under both. If all the strands along one side of the previous row are left unworked, a "bar" of yarn will be left sitting across the work, and the item will have a tendency to fold along this line.

Between the stitches

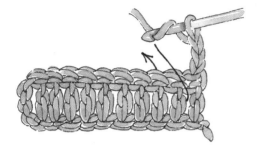

Inserting the hook between 2 stitches will create a fabric that is a little more open than if the stitches were placed one on top of the other. But, if the yarn is heavily textured, it will be much easier to work out exactly where to insert the hook. To work a stitch placed in this way, simply slide the hook through the work, from front to back, between the 2 stitches specified in the pattern.

Into chain spaces

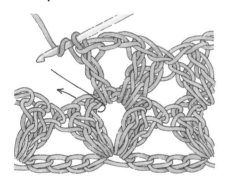

Lacy stitch patterns and motifs often place stitches into a "hole," or chain space, created in the work. When working into a chain space, insert the hook through this "hole," from front to back, and work the stitch so that the entire chain is enclosed by the new stitch.

CREATING A FABRIC

Strings of crochet stitches need to be placed one on top of the other in order to create a fabric, and these strings can either be worked backwards and forwards in rows, or around in circles to form rounds.

Turning chains

However the stitches are positioned to form the fabric, the working loop used for the new stitches is generally on the top of a stitch. So, at the end of one row or round, this working loop needs to be raised up to the top of the stitches that will form the new row or round – and this is done by working a few chain stitches, known as a "turning chain."

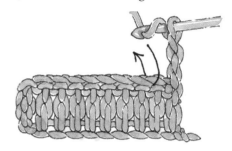

The number of chain stitches that need to be worked varies according to the type of stitches being worked – for example, a double crochet stitch is roughly equal in height to 3 chain stitches, but a single crochet equals just one chain stitch. Throughout this book, each pattern states exactly what must be worked at the beginning and end of each row or round to bring the working loop to the required position for the next set of stitches.

Working in rows

The simplest way to form a crochet fabric is by working backwards and forwards in rows of stitches, with a turning chain at the beginning of each row. The work should be turned at the end of each row, working one row with the right side of the work facing and the following row with the wrong side of the work facing.

Working in rounds

Crochet can also be worked to form circular tubes of crochet, starting with a length of chain that is joined to form a loop, or flat disks, formed by ever-growing rounds worked into a tiny ring of chain stitches.

Each round of crochet is worked in a similar way to a row, but the ends of the rounds are joined, usually by working a slip stitch into the top of the first stitch. Crochet stitches appear different when viewed from the right side than when viewed from the wrong side, so it is advisable to check whether the pattern being followed requires the work to be turned or not at the end of each round. If the item being crocheted combines sections worked in rounds and rows, it is advisable to turn the work at the end of each round to create a fabric that looks the same as the sections worked in rows.

Fastening off

Once each crochet section has been completed, there will still be one stitch on the hook. This stitch should be fastened off by cutting the yarn and drawing this cut end through the final stitch. Pull gently on the end to secure it.

FOLLOWING A CROCHET PATTERN

A crochet pattern should give all the information needed to make the item. Before beginning, it is a good idea to read through the whole pattern to understand exactly how the item will be constructed.

Measurements

This section gives details of what size the item will be when completed and, in the case of a garment, what size person it should fit. Garments normally have a little "ease" added to accommodate a body size larger than they are designed to fit.

Materials

This section of the pattern lists everything needed to make the item – the amount and type of yarn required, the size crochet hook to use and anything else that may be needed to complete the item, such as beads or buttons.

The amounts of yarn stated are based on average requirements and are therefore approximate. If a garment is lengthened or shortened, more or less yarn is needed. Even with modern technology, batches of yarn dyed at separate times can vary very slightly in color and, while not apparent in the ball, this variation can often become very clear once the item is made. It is therefore advisable to buy all the yarn needed to complete the item at the same time, ensuring each ball carries the same "dye lot" number.

Abbreviations

Crochet uses a "shorthand" system to save writing out in full each and every stitch to be worked, abbreviating each stitch type down to just a few letters. Many abbreviations are common to all crochet patterns and these frequently-used abbreviations are all listed here. Sometimes a pattern will use a stitch that is specific to just this one design and a special abbreviation will be given.

Gauge

The gauge section of the design gives the details of the gauge needed to recreate the item photographed. Sometimes the gauge and the hook size specified will be different than expected for that type of yarn in order to create a particular effect for that item.

Making the item

Many crochet patterns are given in more than one size. The amount of stitches or measurements needed for each size are given as lists of numbers in parentheses (). If the second size is being made, then the second set of numbers should be used whenever the parenthetical measurements appear.

If only one number is given, then it should be followed for all sizes. This happens in projects where the exact finished size of the

ABBREVIATIONS

beaded ch – slide bead up next to work, yo and draw loop through leaving bead sitting against RS of work

beaded sc – insert hook as indicated, slide bead up next to work, yo and draw loop through leaving bead sitting against RS of work, yo and draw through both loops on hook

sequined sc – insert hook as indicated, slide sequin up next to work, yo and draw loop through leaving sequin sitting against RS of work, yo and draw through both loops on hook

alt	alternate	mm	millimeters
beg	beginning	patt	pattern
ch	chain	rem	remaining
cm	centimeters	rep(s)	repeat(s)
cont	continue	RS	right side
dc	double crochet	sc	single crochet
dec	decreas(e)(ing)	sp(s)	space(s)
dtr	double treble	sl st	slip stitch
foll	following	st(s)	stitch(es)
hdc	half double crochet	tr(s)	treble(s)
in	inches	WS	wrong side
inc	increas(e)(ing)	yo	yarn over

item being made is not crucial, as with the various accessories featured in the book.

When more than one stitch is to be worked into an area, this group of stitches is shown in parentheses ( ) as a series of stitches. All the stitches in the parentheses should be worked into the place stated after the parentheses.

Occasionally a pattern will require a certain group of stitches be repeated more than once; this group is shown in brackets [ ]. The instructions contained in these brackets should be repeated the number of times stated after the closing bracket.

Crochet stitch patterns often require the same group of stitches be repeated many times across a row or round. A star * appears at the beginning of the series to be repeated. Return to the star to begin the next repeat.

Occasionally there will be a double star ** appearing within a starred series of repeats. The pattern will state that the last repeat of the series should end at this point, ignoring the remaining instructions that were repeated previously. Instructions will then be given for what to do next.

Most crochet items are made in more than one piece; it's a good idea to make these sections in the order given on the pattern. Otherwise, it may be difficult to complete the garment since pieces often refer back to previous sections for certain measurements, or require other pieces to be complete in order to add another section.

Once all sections have been made, the written pattern tells how to then complete the item. It also gives instructions for any edgings or trims to be added. Once again, it is important to follow the order of finishing and joining the pieces so that any extra sections, such as collars, cuffs, and bands can be worked along the correct edges.

Following crochet diagrams

The stitch pattern used for a crochet item can be shown on a diagram. This diagram provides a visual reference of exactly how the stitches that make up the pattern fit together. The diagram uses a different symbol for each type of stitch worked – tall symbols for tall stitches and short symbols for short stitches – with these symbols being placed together as they would be on the finished work. As with abbreviations, certain symbols are common to crochet patterns while some symbols are specific to one particular stitch pattern. Each diagram should be accompanied by a key explaining what each symbol means.

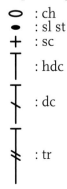

- *Sometimes the beads will "move" through the crochet fabric as rows or rounds are added and you may need to gently ease them back through to the right side of the work once the crochet section has been completed.*
- *Each motif is generally made in the same way as every other motif – but it is a good idea to double check on the pattern that this is the case!*

- *Be careful when placing the first and last stitches of rows of crochet that they are worked into the correct place. If the turning chain is counted as the first stitch of the new row, do NOT work into the stitch at the base of the chain. And, at the ends of rows, make sure to place the last stitch in the top of the turning chain of the previous row if this chain replaced the first stitch.*
- *Take care not to twist the base chain when joining the ends to form the foundation ring as this can make the edge uneven and spoil the work.*

SHAPING WITHIN CROCHET

Not all crochet items are made of simple tubes or strips of crochet, and stitches will need to be increased or decreased to create the final pieces. The pattern instructions usually set out exactly what combination of stitches need to be worked to achieve the shaping while still retaining the stitch pattern.

Decreasing is often achieved in crochet by working two stitches so that they join at the top, forming an upside-down V shape. Each stitch, or "leg", forming this V shape is worked in the normal way up to the last stage. Once both stitches have been worked to this point, the individual stitches, or "legs", are joined by taking the yarn over the hook and drawing this new loop of yarn through all the loops on the hook, thereby joining the two stitches at the top.

WORKING WITH BEADS AND SEQUINS

Many of the items in this book use beads or sequins to create the finished effect, and these are attached while the item is being crocheted.

Using beads

When working with beads, they must be threaded onto the yarn before starting to crochet the pieces. To thread the beads onto the yarn, start by threading a sewing needle with thread, making sure to chose a needle which will easily pass through the beads! Knot the thread ends to form a loop of thread, and slip the cut end of the yarn through this loop. Thread a bead onto the needle, and then gently slide it along the thread and onto the yarn. Continue in this way until the required number of beads are on the yarn.

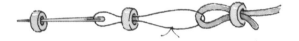

As the crochet is worked, the beads on the yarn should be slipped along the yarn away from the work until they are needed. However, as repeatedly sliding many beads along a delicate yarn can damage the yarn, it is a good idea to thread the beads on in groups of no more than about 200–300 at a time. Once these beads have been used, break the yarn, thread on the same number again and re-join the yarn.

To work a beaded crochet stitch – either a single crochet or a chain stitch – start by sliding a bead up along the yarn so that it rests right next to the last stitch worked. Insert the hook and make the next stitch in the usual way, leaving the bead at the back of the work.

When shaping the edges (such as for an armhole or neck) of a beaded section, take care not to place a bead on the end stitch of a row as this could make it difficult to attach this section to any other section it needs to be seamed to later.

Using sequins

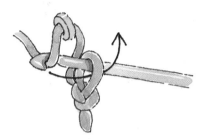

Sequins can be threaded onto the crochet yarn in exactly the same way as beads. Since the holes in sequins are often larger than those in beads, it may be possible to simply thread them directly onto the yarn.

Sequined single crochet and chain stitches are worked in exactly the same way as beaded stitches. Sequins can, however, sometimes fold themselves up the wrong way as they are attached and it may be necessary, once the section is complete, to just gently smooth the sequins down so they all lie in the same direction.

MOTIFS

Some of the designs in this book are made up of lots of small motifs that are joined together to form the finished item. There is often a diagram that will show how these motifs are joined.

The gauge section for a motif will often state the size one finished motif should be, as it is not possible to give a stitch and row gauge. It is vitally important that this motif size be matched exactly if the item is to fit.

Where an item is made up of motifs, the pattern instructions will usually state the shape one motif should be when completed, and give details of what should be around the outer edge of this first motif. Once the first motif has been worked, look closely at it to check that it was done correctly and to identify the features mentioned.

Motifs are usually joined to each other as the last round is worked; the pattern will explain exactly where these joining points should be, and how the motifs should be joined. Join the motifs while working this last round by holding the motif being worked on against the one it is being joined with—their wrong sides together—and work the joining stitch as detailed in the pattern. Follow the diagram, making sure that any extra joining points required in the written instructions are made to complete the item.

WORKING AN EDGING

Crochet items often have a separate edging added afterward to smooth out the edge and give a professional finish. It is important that this edging is worked evenly. It can be very easy to accidentally stretch an edge while working along it and this will distort and spoil the work.

The first row or round of an edging is usually worked with the right side of the crochet facing. To attach the yarn to start an edging, make a slip knot and slip this over the hook. Insert the hook into the edge at the point specified in the pattern and work a slip stitch to secure the yarn. Follow the pattern to work the rest of the edging, taking great care – if working in rounds – to check whether the work needs to be turned or not at the end of each round.

Crab stitch

Almost all crochet stitches are worked from right to left, but there is one common exception to this rule – the crab stitch, also known as the reverse single crochet. This forms a neat corded edging and it is worked from left to right. It is basically just a row of single crochet, but worked backward.

Work a line of crab stitch by inserting the hook into the stitch to the right of the previous stitch, inserting it from front to back and making sure that the yarn is held above the hook and the work. Loop the yarn under the hook and draw this new loop of yarn through the stitch so that there are 2 loops on the hook. Take the yarn over the hook in the usual way and carefully pull this new loop through both loops on the hook to complete the stitch. Continue along the edge, making each stitch in exactly the same way, to form a neat edging that consists of lots of knots along the edge of the work.

JOINING THE CROCHETED PIECES

Once all the crocheted sections have been completed, they may need to be joined together to complete the item. To join the pieces together, use a blunt-pointed sewing needle and the same yarn as used for the crochet. While it is possible to buy needles specifically designed for sewing together hand knits or crochet items, a large-eyed tapestry or cross-stitch embroidery needle is just as good. Using a large blunt-tipped needle ensures that, as the seam is stitched, the fibers of the yarn used are gently eased apart, leaving room for the seaming yarn to easily slide through the work without causing any damage.

The type of stitch that should be used to join the edges together will depend on the type of crochet stitch that has been worked, the yarn that has been used and the position of the seam within the item.

Mattress stitching a seam

A mattress stitch seam creates a flat seam that, depending on the yarn and stitch pattern used, will be virtually invisible. This type of seam is particularly useful when joining fine yarns and lacy stitches.

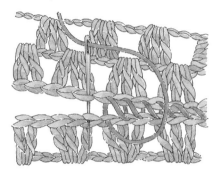

Make the seam by holding the two edges to be joined next to each other, with their right sides facing. Carefully and neatly sew the edges together, making stitches that are about the same size as a chain stitch would be. Once the seam is complete, open out the two pieces and gently flatten the seam.

Back stitching a seam

Back stitching creates a seam that is strong but flexible, making it ideal for shoulder seams on large garments. However, because of the way the seam is made, it can create quite a bulky seam, so is best avoided when working with thick yarns, and can be very difficult to work on very lacy stitch patterns.

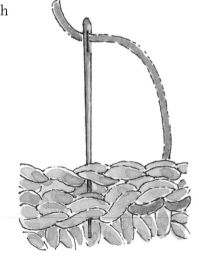

Hold the two sections to be joined with their right sides together and work a line of back stitch along the edge, making each stitch through both layers. Try to work the stitches as close as possible to the edge of the crochet.

Crocheting a seam

Crochet sections can be joined by working a line of single crochet to create the seam. This type of seam is very strong, very flexible and, if worked correctly, will lie virtually flat, not adding any bulk inside the garment.

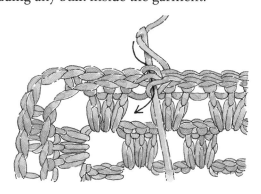

Holding the two pieces to be joined with their right sides together and using the same size hook as used for the main crochet sections, attach the yarn at one end of the seam. Now work a row of single crochet along the edges, inserting the hook through the edges of both sections when working each stitch.

FINISHING THE CROCHET

Once the crochet item is completed, it may need to be ironed. Before ironing the work, refer to the label of the yarn being used to find out exactly how this should be done. This is particularly important when working with the fancy textured and the sparkly yarns featured in this book. Follow the instructions on the yarn label very carefully to avoid damaging the yarn.

Regardless of the ironing instructions on the yarn label, extra care must be taken if the item is decorated with beads or sequins. Even a warm iron will melt sequins, and fragile glass beads could easily shatter if they come in contact with an iron.

If the beads are small and the yarn can be ironed, iron the item very carefully from the wrong side of the work, protecting the beads by covering the surface with layers of soft cloth to cushion them – a couple of soft towels covered with an old sheet are ideal. Using a pressing cloth avoids the risk of the iron damaging a stray bead that may have crept through to the wrong side of the work.

If the item has sequins, do NOT iron it! If it does need to be "pressed," it can be blocked out to size. To block out the item, cover a large firm surface, such as an old table, with several towels under an old sheet or tablecloth. Pin the item out to shape on this surface, making sure that all the sequins "lie" in their correct positions and that the item is the size detailed in the pattern. Cover the pinned-out work with another cloth and mist this cloth with water – it should be damp, not wet! Leave everything to dry naturally away from direct heat. Once totally dry, remove the cloth and the pins and the item is complete.

AFTERCARE

It is a good idea to keep a small amount of the yarn used, together with its label and a few spare beads or sequins, in a safe place so that they can be referred to at a later date. The yarn label will give details of how the yarn should be laundered but, if beads or sequins are attached, the item should NOT be machine washed even if the yarn could be. Instead, hand wash the item very carefully in lukewarm water or have it dry cleaned by a professional.

BRIGHT LIGHTS

Light up a dark evening with these dynamic designs worked
in myriad bright jewel tone colors. Yarns in passionate pinks,
gorgeous greens, perfect purple, terrific turquoise, glittering
gold and ruby red are sure to get you noticed. Some designs
are intricately encrusted with beads and others are really
simple and quick to make – but all of them are sure to
bring smiles.

Keep cozy and warm but still look stunning in this little edge-to-edge jacket. Short and boxy, it will work up quick in a really chunky and luscious chenille yarn – and the little loops create the cutest of ringlets!

"Fur" Jacket

 INTERMEDIATE

MEASUREMENTS

To fit bust

32	34	36	38	40	42	in
81	86	91	97	102	107	cm

Actual size

$34^1/_2$	37	$39^1/_4$	$41^3/_4$	44	$46^1/_2$	in
88	94	100	106	112	118	cm

Actual length

$16^1/_2$	17	$17^1/_4$	$17^3/_4$	18	$18^1/_2$	in
42	43	44	45	46	47	cm

Actual sleeve

17	17	$17^1/_4$	$17^1/_4$	$17^1/_4$	$17^3/_4$	in
43	43	44	44	44	45	cm

MATERIALS

- 8 (9: 9: 9: 10: 11) of Lion Brand Chenille Thick and Quick in Raspberry 112
- N/15 (10.00) mm crochet hook

GAUGE

$6^1/_2$ sts and $6^1/_2$ rows to 4 in (10 cm) measured over pattern using N/15 hook. Change hook size if necessary to obtain this gauge.

ABBREVIATIONS

sc2tog – *insert hook as indicated, yo and draw loop through, rep from * once more, yo and draw through all 3 loops on hook;

loop 1=insert hook into next st, using finger of left hand draw out yarn to form a loop approx 4–$4^1/_2$ in (10–12 cm) long, pick up both strands of this loop with hook and draw through st, yo and draw loop through all 3 loops on hook. *See also page 15.*

BODY (worked in one piece to armholes)

With N/15 hook, ch 58 (62: 66: 70: 74: 78).
Foundation row: (RS) 1 sc into 2nd ch from hook, 1 sc into each ch to end, turn. 57 (61: 65: 69: 73: 77) sts.
Cont in patt as follows:
Row 1: (WS) 1 ch (does NOT count as st), loop 1 into each sc to end, turn.
Row 2: 1 ch (does NOT count as st), 1 sc into each st to end, turn.
These 2 rows form patt.
Cont in patt until Body measures approx $8^1/_4$ ($8^1/_2$: $8^1/_2$: 9: 9: $9^1/_2$) in, 21 (22: 22: 23: 23: 24) cm, ending with a WS row.

Divide for armholes

Next row: (RS) 1 ch (does NOT count as st), 1 sc into each of first 12 (13: 14: 15: 16: 17) sts and turn, leaving rem sts unworked.
Work on this set of 12 (13: 14: 15: 16: 17) sts only for Right Front.

■ *Sirdar Wow! is a really chunky chenille yarn that means your crochet will grow surprisingly quickly – so your jacket will be made faster than you think.*
■ *The fronts and back of this jacket are worked all in one piece so you have fewer seams to sew up. It also means there are no bulky side seams to spoil the look of your finished garment.*

Next row: 1 ch (does NOT count as st), sc2tog over first 2 sts – 1 st decreased, loop 1 into each sc to end, turn.

Next row: 1 ch (does NOT count as st), 1 sc into each st to last 2 sts, sc2tog over last 2 sts – 1 st decreased, turn. 10 (11: 12: 13: 14: 15) sts.

Working all decreases as set by last 2 rows, dec 1 st at armhole edge on next 0 (0: 1: 1: 2: 2) rows. 10 (11: 11: 12: 12: 13) sts.

Cont even until armhole measures approx 5 (5: 5¹/₂: 5¹/₂: 6: 6) in, 13 (13: 14: 14: 15: 15) cm, ending with a RS row.

Shape neck

Next row: (WS) 1 ch (does NOT count as st), loop 1 into each of first 7 (8: 8: 8: 8: 9) sc and turn, leaving rem 3 (3: 3: 4: 4: 4) sts unworked.

Dec 1 st at neck edge on next 2 rows. 5 (6: 6: 6: 6: 7) sts.

Cont even until armhole measures approx 8¹/₄ (8¹/₄: 8¹/₂: 8¹/₂: 9: 9) in, 21 (21: 22: 22: 23: 23) cm, ending with a WS row.

Shape shoulder

Fasten off.

Return to last complete row worked, skip next 4 sts, rejoin yarn to next st and cont as follows:

Next row: (RS) 1 ch (does NOT count as st), 1 sc into st where yarn was rejoined, 1 sc into each of next 24 (26: 28: 30: 32: 34) sts and turn, leaving rem sts unworked.

Work on this set of 25 (27: 29: 31: 33: 35) sts only for back.

Dec 1 st at each end of next 2 (2: 3: 3: 4: 4) rows. 21 (23: 23: 25: 25: 27) sts.

Cont even until back matches right front to shoulder, ending with a WS row.

Shape shoulders

Fasten off, placing markers either side of center 11 (11: 11: 13: 13: 13) sts to denote back neck.

Return to last complete row worked, skip next 4 sts, rejoin yarn to next st and cont as follows:

Next row: (RS) 1 ch (does NOT count as st), 1 sc into st where yarn was rejoined, 1 sc into each st to end, turn.

Work on this set of 12 (13: 14: 15: 16: 17) sts for Left Front.

Dec 1 st at armhole edge on next 2 (2: 3: 3: 4: 4) rows. 10 (11: 11: 12: 12: 13) sts.

Cont even until armhole measures approx 5 (5: 5¹/₂: 5¹/₂: 6: 6) in, 13 (13: 14: 14: 15: 15) cm, ending with a RS row.

Shape neck

Next row: (WS) sl st across and into 4th (4th: 4th: 5th: 5th: 5th) sc, 1 ch (does NOT count as st), loop 1 into same place as last sl st, loop 1 into each sc to end, turn. 7 (8: 8: 8: 8: 9) sts.

Dec 1 st at neck edge on next 2 rows. 5 (6: 6: 6: 6: 7) sts.

Cont even until left front matches right front to shoulder, ending with a WS row.

- *Using Sirdar Wow! for a loop stitch pattern like this one means that all the loops will naturally fall into little ringlets. If you find one or two don't, then simply twist them so that they do!*
- *You might find it difficult to sew up the garment with a yarn this thick. If so, simply sew it up using a matching shade of a thinner yarn.*
- *As there are no edgings added to this garment, it's a good idea to try to keep the front opening and neck edges as neat as possible.*

Shape shoulder
Fasten off.

SLEEVES

With N/15 hook, ch 17 (17: 18: 18: 19: 19).
Work foundation row as given for body. 16 (16: 17: 17: 18: 18) sts.
Cont in patt as given for body as follows:
Work 3 rows, ending with a WS row.
Next row: (RS) 1 ch (does NOT count as st), 2 sc into first sc – 1 st increased, 1 sc into each st to last st, 2 sc into last st – 1 st increased, turn.
Working all increases as set by last row, inc 1 st at each end of every foll 6th row until there are 24 (24: 25: 25: 26: 26) sts.
Cont even until sleeve measures approx 17 (17: $17^1/_4$: $17^1/_4$: $17^1/_4$: $17^3/_4$) in, 43 (43: 44: 44: 44: 45) cm, ending with a RS row.

Shape top
Next row: (WS) sl st across and into 3rd sc, 1 ch (does NOT count as st), loop 1 into same place as last sl st, loop 1 into each of next 19 (19: 20: 20: 21: 21) sc and turn, leaving rem 2 sc unworked.
Dec 1 st at each end of next 7 rows, ending with a RS row. 6 (6: 7: 7: 8: 8) sts.
Fasten off.

FINISHING

Do NOT iron.
Join shoulder seams. Join sleeve seams.
Matching top of sleeve seam to center of sts skipped at underarm and center of last row of sleeve to shoulder seam, sew sleeves into armholes.

This light-as-air shrug will keep chilly breezes off your shoulders. It's worked in a pretty lacy stitch, using the most luxurious of kid mohair and silk blend yarns, and the edges are finished with a neat line of beads.

Shoulder Shrug

INTERMEDIATE

MEASUREMENTS

To fit bust

32–34	36–38	40–42	in
81–86	91–97	102–107	cm

Actual width, at widest point

26³/₄	28³/₄	30³/₄	in
68	73	78	cm

Actual length

16	17	17	in
41	43	45	cm

MATERIALS

- 3 (4: 4) × 1 oz (25 g) balls of Rowan Kidsilk Haze in Splendour 579
- C/2 (2.50 mm) crochet hook
- Approx 210 (220: 230) beads

GAUGE

4 patt reps and 11 rows to 4 in (10 cm) measured over pattern using C/2 hook. Change hook size if necessary to obtain this gauge.

ABBREVIATIONS

See page 15.

For how to work with beads, see pages 16–17.

BACK

With C/2 hook, ch 146 (162: 178).

Foundation row: (RS) 1 sc into 2nd ch from hook, *skip 3 ch, (1 dc, 1 ch, 1 dc, 3 ch, 1 dc, 1 ch and 1 dc) into next ch, skip 3 ch, 1 sc into next ch, rep from * to end, turn. 18 (20: 22) patt reps.

Cont in patt as follows:

Row 1: (WS) 7 ch (count as first dc and 3 ch), skip (1 sc, 1 dc, 1 ch and 1 dc), *(1 sc, 3 ch and 1 sc) into next ch sp, 3 ch, skip (1 dc, 1 ch and 1 dc), 1 tr into next sc**, 3 ch, skip (1 dc, 1 ch and 1 dc), rep from * to end, ending last rep at **, turn.

Row 2: 4 ch (count as first dc and 1 ch), (1 dc, 1 ch and 1 dc) into tr at base of 4 ch, *skip (3 ch and 1 sc), 1 sc into next ch sp, skip (1 sc and 3 ch)**, (1 dc, 1 ch, 1 dc, 3 ch, 1 dc, 1 ch and 1 dc) into next tr, rep from * to end, ending last rep at **, (1 dc, 1 ch, 1 dc, 1 ch and 1 dc) into 4th of 7 ch at beg of previous row, turn.

Row 3: 1 ch (does NOT count as st), 1 sc into dc at end of previous row, 1 sc into next ch sp, *3 ch, skip (1 dc, 1 ch and 1 dc), 1 tr into next sc, 3 ch, skip (1 dc, 1 ch and 1 dc)**, (1 sc, 3 ch and 1 sc) into next ch sp, rep from * to end, ending last rep at **, 1 sc into next ch sp, 1 sc into 3rd of 4 ch at beg of previous row, turn.

■ Designed just to cover your shoulders, this little shrug is the perfect accompaniment to a strappy dress or top. And it's made using such a lightweight yarn that you'll hardly even notice you've got it on!

■ Don't worry if the finished edges don't look totally straight – once the beaded edging is complete, they will straighten out.

Row 4: 1 ch (does NOT count as st), 1 sc into sc at end of previous row, *skip (1 sc and 3 ch), (1 dc, 1 ch, 1 dc, 3 ch, 1 dc, 1 ch and 1 dc) into next tr, skip (3 ch and 1 sc), 1 sc into next ch sp, rep from * to end, working last sc into sc at beg of previous row, turn. These 4 rows form patt. Work 1 row, ending with patt row 1 and a WS row.

Shape sleeve

Next row: (RS) 4 ch (count as first dc and 1 ch), (1 dc, 3 ch, 1 dc, 1 ch and 1 dc) into tr at base of 4 ch - 1/2 patt rep increased, *skip (3 ch and 1 sc), 1 sc into next ch sp, skip (1 sc and 3 ch)**, (1 dc, 1 ch, 1 dc, 3 ch, 1 dc, 1 ch and 1 dc) into next tr, rep from * to end, ending last rep at **, (1 dc, 1 ch, 1 dc, 3 ch, 1 dc, 1 ch and 1 dc) into 4th of 7 ch at beg of previous row – 1/2 patt rep increased, turn.

Next row: 7 ch (count as first tr and 3 ch), skip (1 dc, 1 ch and 1 dc), *(1 sc, 3 ch and 1 sc) into next ch sp, 3 ch**, skip (1 dc, 1 ch and 1 dc), 1 tr into next sc, 3 ch, skip (1 dc, 1 ch and 1 dc), rep from * to end, ending last rep at **, skip (1 dc and 1 ch), 1 tr into 3rd of 4 ch at beg of previous row, turn.

Rep last 2 rows 8 times more. 27 (29: 31) patt reps.

Place markers at both ends of last row to denote base of armhole opening.

Starting with patt row 2, work in patt for a further 19 (21: 23) rows, ending with patt row 4 (2: 4) and a RS row.

First and third sizes only

Next row: (WS) 7 ch (count as first tr and 3 ch), skip (1 sc, 1 dc, 1 ch and 1 dc), *1 sc into next ch sp, 3 ch, skip (1 dc, 1 ch and 1 dc), 1 tr into next sc**, 3 ch, skip (1 dc, 1 ch and 1 dc), rep from * to end, ending last rep at **.

Second size only

Next row: (WS) 1 ch (does NOT count as st), 1 sc into dc at end of previous row, 1 sc into next ch sp, *3 ch, skip (1 dc, 1 ch and 1 dc), 1 tr into next sc, 3 ch, skip (1 dc, 1 ch and 1 dc)**, 1 sc into next ch sp, rep from * to end, ending last rep at **, 1 sc into next ch sp, 1 sc into 3rd of 4 ch at beg of previous row.

All sizes

Fasten off, placing markers either side of center 7 (8: 9) patt reps to denote back neck.

LEFT FRONT

With C/2 hook, ch 10.
Work foundation row as given for back.
1 patt rep.
Starting with patt row 1, cont in patt as given for back as follows:
Work 1 row, ending with patt row 1 and a WS row.

Shape front opening edge

Working all shaping as given for back, inc 1/2 patt rep at end of next and foll alt row. 2 patt reps.
Work 1 row. (6 rows completed.)

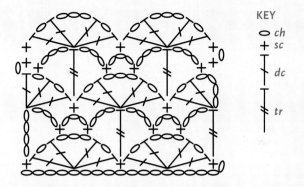

KEY

◦ ch
+ sc
╎ dc
╪ tr

Shape sleeve

Inc $1/2$ patt rep at beg of next and foll alt row. 3 patt reps.

Work 1 row.

Inc $1/2$ patt rep at each end of next and foll alt row. 5 patt reps.

Work 1 row.

Rep last 8 rows once more. 8 patt reps.

Inc $1/2$ patt rep at beg of next row. $8^1/2$ patt reps.

Work 1 row.

Place marker at end of last row to denote base of armhole opening.

Work 2 rows.

Now keeping armhole opening edge straight, inc $1/2$ patt rep at front opening edge of next and foll alt row. $9^1/2$ patt reps.

Work 5 rows.

Second and third sizes only

Rep last 8 rows once more. $10^1/2$ patt reps.

First and third sizes only

Inc $1/2$ patt rep at end of next row. 10 (11) patt reps.

All sizes

Work 9 (4: 5) rows, replacing the (1 sc, 3 ch and 1 sc) into ch sp with (1 sc) as given for last row of back. Fasten off.

RIGHT FRONT

Work as given for left front, reversing all shaping.

FINISHING

Do NOT iron.

Join shoulder/overarm seams. Join side seams below markers.

Edging

Thread beads onto yarn.

With C/2 hook, rejoin yarn at base of one side seam, 1 ch (does NOT count as st), work 1 round of sc evenly around entire hem, front opening and neck edges, ending with sl st to first sc and ensuring number of sts worked is divisible by 4, **turn.**

Next round: (WS) 1 ch (does NOT count as st), 1 sc into first sc, *1 beaded sc into next sc, 1 sc into each of next 3 sc, rep from * to last 3 sc, 1 beaded sc into next sc, 1 sc into each of last 2 sc, sl st to first sc.

Fasten off.

Work edging around armhole opening edges in same way, rejoining yarn at top of side seam.

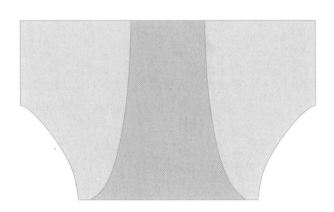

This poncho is really simple to make – it's just sixteen big and lacy motifs! Worked in a stunning hand-dyed ribbon yarn, it'll definitely make you the belle of the ball.

Poncho

EASY

MEASUREMENTS

One size, to fit bust
34–42 in
86–107 cm

Actual size, at widest point
33¹/₂ in
85 cm

Actual length, from nape of neck
28 in
71 cm

MATERIALS

- 3 × 3¹/₂ oz (100g) hanks of Colinette Giotto in Rio 140
- K/10.5 (7.00 mm) crochet hook

GAUGE

Motif measures 7³/₄ in (20 cm) square on K/10.5 hook. Change hook size if necessary to obtain this gauge.

ABBREVIATIONS

dc2tog – *yo and insert hook as indicated, yo and draw loop through, yo and draw through 2 loops, rep from * once more, yo and draw through all 3 loops on hook; **dc3tog** – *yo and insert hook as indicated, yo and draw loop through, yo and draw through 2 loops, rep from * twice more, yo and draw through all 4 loops on hook. *See also page 15.*

MOTIF

With K/10.5 hook, ch 6 and join with a sl st to form a ring.
Round 1: (RS) 1 ch (does NOT count as st), [1 sc into ring, 15 ch] 12 times, sl st to first sc. 12 ch sps.
Round 2: sl st into each of first 7 ch of first ch sp, 3 ch (do NOT count as st), (dc2tog, 4 ch and dc3tog) into same ch sp, *[4 ch, 1 sc into next ch sp] twice, 4 ch**, (dc3tog, 4 ch and dc3tog) into next ch sp, rep from * to end, ending last rep at **, sl st to top of dc2tog at beg of round.
Round 3: sl st into first ch sp, 3 ch (do NOT count as st), (dc2tog, 5 ch and dc3tog) into same ch sp, *5 ch, 1 sc into next ch sp, 5 ch, dc3tog into next ch sp, 5 ch, 1 sc into next ch sp, 5 ch**, (dc3tog, 5 ch and dc3tog) into next ch sp, rep from * to end, ending last rep at **, sl st to top of dc2tog at beg of round.
Fasten off.
Basic Motif is a square. In each corner there is a 5-ch sp between a pair of dc3tog, and along sides there are a further four 5-ch sps. Join Motifs while working Round 3 at corners, by replacing corner (5 ch) with (2 ch, 1 sl st into corner 5-ch sp of adjacent motif, 2 ch), and at side ch sps, by replacing (5 ch) with (2 ch, 1 sl st into corresponding ch sp of adjacent motif, 2 ch).

- *Quick and easy to make, this poncho will look just as great over a T-shirt and jeans as with the most elegant of evening dresses.*
- *Colinette Giotto is a hand-dyed ribbon yarn and, as every batch of yarn is dyed individually, your garment will be totally unique.*
- *The instructions are given for the motifs to be joined to each other as they are made, but there is no reason why, if you prefer, they cannot be made separately and sewn together later.*

- *To save weaving in the yarn end at the center of each motif, work over it when making the first round so that it is totally enclosed. Once the motif is completed, you can simply snip off the visible end and there's nothing else to weave in!*

Following diagram, make and join 16 basic motifs to form shape shown. Join second overarm/side seam while joining motifs as indicated by arrows.

Neck Edging

With K/10.5 hook and RS facing, attach yarn at point A on diagram and work around neck edge as follows: 1 ch (does NOT count as st), 1 sc into joining point of motifs – this is where yarn was rejoined, *2 ch, 1 sc into next ch sp, [3 ch, 1 sc into next ch sp] 3 times, 2 ch, 1 sc into next joining point, rep from * to end, replacing sc at end of last rep with sl st to first sc, turn.

Next round: (WS) 1 ch (does NOT count as st), 2 sc into first ch sp, *[1 sc into next sc, 3 sc into next ch sp] 3 times, 1 sc into next sc, 2 sc into next ch sp, skip next sc, rep from * to end, sl st to first sc.

Fasten off.

FINISHING

Do NOT iron.

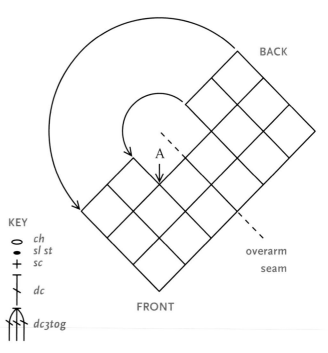

KEY

○	ch
•	sl st
+	sc
dc symbol	dc
dc3tog symbol	dc3tog

Knock 'em dead in this sexy little top! Made in a delicate openwork lacy stitch using a shimmering kid mohair yarn with a touch of Lurex®, the edges are trimmed with glittering beads to complete the look.

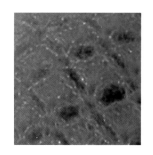

Tie Front Cardigan

INTERMEDIATE

MEASUREMENTS

To fit bust

30–32	32–34	36–38	38–40	42–44	in
76–81	81–86	91–97	97–102	107–112	cm

Actual size

$33^{1}/_2$	$36^{1}/_2$	$39^{3}/_4$	$42^{1}/_2$	$45^{1}/_2$	in
85	93	101	108	116	cm

Actual length

$20^{1}/_2$	$20^{1}/_2$	$20^{3}/_4$	$21^{1}/_2$	$21^{1}/_2$	in
52	52	53	55	55	cm

Actual sleeve

18	18	18	18	18	in
46	46	46	46	46	cm

MATERIALS

- 6 (7: 8: 9: 10) × 1 oz (25 g) balls of Rowan Kidsilk Night in Dazzle 609
- E/4 (3.50 mm) crochet hook
- Approx 510 (520: 560: 600: 620) beads

GAUGE

26 sts and 13 rows to 4 in (10 cm) measured over pattern using E/4 hook. Change hook size if necessary to obtain this gauge.

ABBREVIATIONS

See page 15.

For how to work with beads, see pages 16–17.

BACK

With E/4 hook, ch 112 (122: 132: 142: 152).

Foundation row: (RS) 1 sc into 2nd ch from hook, 1 sc into next ch, *skip 3 ch, (3 dc, 1 ch and 3 dc) into next ch, skip 3 ch, 1 sc into next ch**, 1 ch, skip 1 ch, 1 sc into next ch, rep from * to end, ending last rep at **, 1 sc into last ch, turn. 111 (121: 131: 141: 151) sts, 11 (12: 13: 14: 15) patt reps.

Cont in patt as follows:

Row 1: (WS) 2 ch (count as first hdc), 1 hdc into sc at base of 2 ch, *3 ch, skip (1 sc and 3 dc), 1 sc into next ch sp, 3 ch, skip (3 dc and 1 sc)**, (1 hdc, 1 ch and 1 hdc) into next ch sp, rep from * to end, ending last rep at **, 2 hdc into last sc, turn.

Row 2: 3 ch (count as first dc), 3 dc into hdc at base of 3 ch, *skip 1 hdc, 1 sc into next ch sp, 1 ch, skip 1 sc, 1 sc into next ch sp, skip 1 hdc**, (3 dc, 1 ch and 3 dc) into next ch sp, rep from * to end, ending last rep at **, 4 dc into top of 2 ch at beg of previous row, turn.

Row 3: 1 ch (does NOT count as st), 1 sc into last dc of previous row, *3 ch, skip (3 dc and 1 sc), (1 hdc, 1 ch and 1 hdc) into next ch sp, 3 ch, skip (1 sc and 3 dc), 1 sc into next ch sp, rep from * to end, working sc at end of last rep into top of 3 ch at beg of previous row, turn.

Row 4: 1 ch (does NOT count as st), 1 sc into sc at end of previous row, *1 sc into next ch sp, skip 1 hdc, (3 dc, 1 ch and 3 dc) into next ch sp, skip 1 hdc, 1 sc into next ch sp**, 1 ch, skip 1 sc, rep from * to end, ending last rep at **, 1 sc into last sc, turn.

These 4 rows form patt.

Cont in patt for a further 36 rows, ending with patt row 4 and a RS row. (Back should measure 12^1/$_2$ in, 32 cm.)

Shape armholes

Next row: (WS) sl st across first 2 sc, next 3 dc and into next ch sp, 1 ch (does NOT count as st), 1 sc into same ch sp as last sl st - ^{1}/$_2$ patt rep decreased, *3 ch, skip (3 dc and 1 sc), (1 hdc, 1 ch and 1 hdc) into next ch sp, 3 ch, skip (1 sc and 3 dc), 1 sc into next ch sp, rep from * until sc has been worked into ch sp between last group of trs and turn, leaving rem (3 dc and 2 sc) unworked – ^{1}/$_2$ patt rep decreased.

Next row: As patt row 4.

Rep last 2 rows 2 (2: 3: 3: 4) times more. 8 (9: 9: 10: 10) patt reps.

Work a further 19 (19: 19: 21: 19) rows, ending with a WS row. (Armhole should measure 7^1/$_2$ (7^1/$_2$: 8: 8^1/$_2$: 8^1/$_2$) in, 19 (19: 20: 22: 22) cm. Fasten off, placing markers 2 (2^1/$_2$: 2^1/$_2$: 2^1/$_2$: 2^1/$_2$) patt reps in from each end of last row to denote back neck – there should be 4 (4: 4: 5: 5) patt reps across back neck.

LEFT FRONT

With E/4 hook, ch 162 (172: 182: 192: 202). Work foundation row as given for Back. 161 (171: 181: 191: 201) sts, 16 (17: 18: 19: 20) patt reps.

Cont in patt as given for back follows:

Work 4 rows, ending with patt row 4 and a RS row.

Shape tie

Working all shaping as given for Back, dec ^{1}/$_2$ patt rep at beg of next row. 15^1/$_2$ (16^1/$_2$: 17^1/$_2$: 18^1/$_2$: 19^1/$_2$) patt reps.

Dec 4 patt reps at end of next row (by simply leaving last 4 patt reps unworked – row should end in same way as patt row 4 ends). 11^1/$_2$ (12^1/$_2$: 13^1/$_2$: 14^1/$_2$: 15^1/$_2$) patt reps.

Dec ^{1}/$_2$ patt rep at beg of next and foll 9 (11: 12: 14: 16) alt rows, then on 2 (1: 1: 0: 0) foll 6th rows. 5^1/$_2$ (6: 6^1/$_2$: 7: 7) patt reps.

***Work 3 (5: 3: 5: 1) rows. (Left front should now match back to start of armhole shaping.)

Shape armhole

Dec ^{1}/$_2$ patt rep at armhole edge of next and foll 2 (2: 3: 3: 4) alt rows and at same time dec ^{1}/$_2$ patt rep at front slope edge on 3rd (next: 3rd: next: 5th) and foll 0 (0: 0: 6th: 0) row. 3^1/$_2$ (4: 4: 4: 4) patt reps.

Dec ^{1}/$_2$ patt rep at front slope edge only on 4th (2nd: 2nd: 6th: 2nd) and every foll 6th row until 2 (2^1/$_2$: 2^1/$_2$: 2^1/$_2$: 2^1/$_2$) patt reps rem.

Work a further 4 (6: 6: 4: 6) rows, ending with

a WS row. (Left Front should match Back to fasten-off row.)
Fasten off.

RIGHT FRONT

Work as given for Left Front to start of tie shaping.

Shape tie

Working all shaping as given for Back, dec 1/2 patt rep at end of next row. 15¹/₂ (16¹/₂: 17¹/₂: 18¹/₂: 19¹/₂) patt reps.

Dec 4 patt reps at beg of next row (by simply breaking yarn and re-joining it 4 patt reps further along row – row should begin in same way as patt row 4 begins). 11¹/₂ (12¹/₂: 13¹/₂: 14¹/₂: 15¹/₂) patt reps.

Dec 1/2 patt rep at end of next and foll 9 (11: 12: 14: 16) alt rows, then on 2 (1: 1: 0: 0) foll 6th rows. 5¹/₂ (6: 6¹/₂: 7: 7) patt reps.

Complete as given for left front from ***.

SLEEVES

With E/4 hook, ch 52 (52: 62: 72: 72).

Work foundation row as given for back. 51 (51: 61: 71: 71) sts, 5 (5: 6: 7: 7) patt reps.

Cont in patt as given for back follows:

Work 9 rows, ending with patt row 1 and a WS row.

Next row: (RS) 3 ch (count as first dc), (3 dc, 1 ch and 3 dc) into hdc at base of 3 ch, *skip 1 hdc, 1 sc into next ch sp, 1 ch, skip 1 sc, 1 sc into next ch sp, skip 1 hdc**, (3 dc, 1 ch and 3 dc) into next ch sp, rep from * to end, ending last rep at **, (3 dc, 1 ch and 4 dc) into top of 2 ch at beg of previous row, turn.

Next row: 2 ch (count as first hdc), 1hdc into dc at base of 2 ch – 1/2 patt rep increased, 3 ch, skip 3 dc, *1 sc into next ch sp, 3 ch**, skip (3 dc and 1 sc), (1 hdc, 1 ch and 1 hdc) into next ch sp, 3 ch, skip (1 sc and 3 dc), rep from * to end, ending last rep at **, skip 3 dc, 2 hdc into top of 3 ch at beg of previous row – 1/2 patt rep increased, turn. 6 (6: 7: 8: 8) patt reps.

Starting with patt row 2, work 12 rows, ending with patt row 1 and a RS row.

Rep last 14 rows twice more. 8 (8: 9: 10: 10) patt reps.

Work a further 7 rows, ending with patt row 4 and a WS row. (Sleeve should measure 17³/₄ in, 45 cm.)

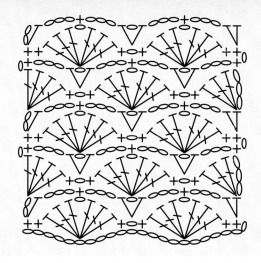

KEY
o   ch
+   sc
⊤   hdc
†️   dc

Shape top

Working all shaping as given for back, dec ½ patt rep at each end of next and foll 5 (5: 6: 7: 7) alt rows. 2 patt reps.
Fasten off.

FINISHING

Do NOT iron.
Join shoulder and side seams. Join sleeve seams. Sew sleeves into armholes.

Edging

Thread beads onto yarn.
With E/4 hook, rejoin yarn at base of one side seam, 1 ch (does NOT count as st), work
1 round of sc evenly around entire hem, tie, front opening and neck edges, ending with sl st to first sc and ensuring an even number of sts are worked, **turn**.
Next round: (WS) 1 ch (does NOT count as st), *1 sc into next sc, 1 beaded sc into next sc, rep from * to end, sl st to first sc, turn.
Next round: 1 ch (does NOT count as st), 1 sc into each st to end, sl st to first sc.
Fasten off.
Work edging around lower edge of sleeves in same way, rejoining yarn at base of sleeve seam.

This little funnel-neck top, with its cut-away armholes, is gently fitted to flatter your figure. Made with a fine Lurex® yarn, it uses a clever textured stitch that is easy to work. And it looks just as good with jeans as with the dressiest of skirts.

Sleeveless Top

 INTERMEDIATE

MEASUREMENTS

To fit bust

32	34	36	38	40	42	in
81	86	91	97	102	107	cm

Actual size, at underarm

33¹/₂	34¹/₂	37¹/₂	39	41¹³/₄	43¹/₄	in
85	88	95	99	106	110	cm

Actual length

20¹/₂	20³/₄	22¹/₂	22¹/₂	23¹/₄	23¹/₂	in
52	53	55	57	59	60	cm

MATERIALS

● 28 (28: 32: 36: 36: 40) × 1³/₄ oz (50 g) balls of Lion Brand Glitterspun in Amethyst 144
● C/2 (2.50 mm) crochet hook

GAUGE

34 sts and 17 rows to 4 in (10 cm) measured over pattern using C/2 hook. Change hook size if necessary to obtain this gauge.

ABBREVIATIONS

See page 15.

BACK

With C/2 hook, ch 146 (152: 164: 170: 182: 188).
Foundation row: (RS) 1 sc into 2nd ch from hook, *skip 2 ch, (1 dc, 1 ch, 1 dc, 1 ch and 1 dc) into next ch, skip 2 ch, 1 sc into next ch, rep from * to end, turn. 145 (151: 163: 169: 181: 187) sts, 24 (25: 27: 28: 30: 31) patt reps.
Cont in patt as follows:
Row 1: (WS) 4 ch (count as 1 dc and 1 ch), 1 dc into sc at base of 4 ch, *skip (1 dc and 1 ch), 1 sc into next dc, skip (1 ch and 1 dc)**, (1 dc, 1 ch, 1 dc, 1 ch and 1 dc) into next sc, rep from * to end, ending last rep at **, (1 dc, 1 ch and 1 dc) into last sc, turn.
Row 2: 1 ch (does NOT count as st), 1 sc into dc at end of previous row, *skip (1 ch and 1 dc), (1 dc, 1 ch, 1 dc, 1 ch and 1 dc) into next sc, skip (1 dc and 1 ch), 1 sc into next dc, rep from * to end, working sc at end of last rep into 3rd of 4 ch at beg of previous row, turn.
These 2 rows form patt.
Keeping patt correct, cont as follows:
Work 2 rows, ending with a RS row.
Next row: (WS) sl st across (first sc, 1 dc, 1 ch) and into next dc, 1 ch (does NOT count as st), 1 sc into dc at base of 1 ch – ¹/₂ patt rep decreased. Work in patt until sc has been worked into dc at center of last patt rep and

turn, leaving (1 ch, 1 dc and 1 sc) unworked – $^1/_2$ patt rep decreased. 23 (24: 26: 27: 29: 30) patt reps.

Working all decreases as set by last row, dec $^1/_2$ patt rep at each end of 5th and foll 5th row. 21 (22: 24: 25: 27: 28) patt reps.

Work 12 rows, ending with patt row 2.

Next row: 3 ch (count as first st), (1 dc, 1 ch, 1 dc, 1 ch and 1 dc) into sc at base of 3 ch – $^1/_2$ patt rep increased, work in patt to end, working (1 dc, 1 ch, 1 dc, 1 ch and **2** dc) into last sc – $^1/_2$ patt rep increased, turn. 22 (23: 25: 26: 28: 29) patt reps.

Next row: 4 ch (count as 1 dc and 1 ch), 1 dc into **dc** at base of 4 ch, *skip (1 dc and 1 ch), 1 sc into next dc, skip (1 ch and 1 dc)**, (1 dc, 1 ch, 1 dc, 1 ch and 1 dc) into next sc, rep from * to end, ending last rep at **, (1 dc, 1 ch and 1 dc) into top of 3 ch at beg of previous row, turn.

Working all increases as now set, cont as follows:
Work 5 rows.

Inc $^1/_2$ patt rep at each end of next and foll 7th row. 24 (25: 27: 28: 30: 31) patt reps.

Cont even until back measures 13 in, 33 cm, ending with patt row 2.

Shape armholes

Dec $^1/_2$ patt rep at each end of next and every foll 3rd row until 85 (85: 91: 91: 97: 97) sts, 14 (14: 15: 15: 16: 16) patt reps rem.

Work 2 rows.

Fasten off, placing markers either side of center 59 (59: 65: 65: 71: 71) sts to denote back neck.

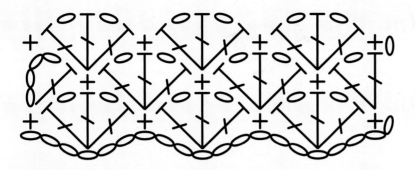

FRONT

Work as given for back until 103 (103: 109: 109: 115: 115) sts, 17 (17: 18: 18: 19: 19) patt reps rem in armhole shaping.

Shape neck

Next row: Work in patt 31 sts and turn, leaving rem sts unworked.

Work 1 row.

Dec $^{1}/_{2}$ patt rep at each end of next and every foll 3rd row until 13 sts, 2 patt reps rem.

Work 2 rows.

Fasten off.

Return to last complete row worked, skip center 41 (41: 47: 47: 53: 53) sts, rejoin yarn to next st, 4 ch (count as 1 dc and 1 ch), 1 dc into sc at base of 4 ch, patt to end. 31 sts. Complete to match first side.

FINISHING

Do NOT iron.

Join left shoulder seam.

Neck border

With RS facing and C/2 hook, rejoin yarn at right neck shoulder point of back, 4 ch (count as 1 dc and 1 ch), 1 dc into sc at base of 4 ch, work until 10 (10: 11: 11: 12: 12) patt reps have been completed across back neck as set, 3 patt reps down left side of front neck, 7 (7: 8: 8: 9: 9) patt reps across front as set, then 3 patt reps up right side of neck, turn. 23 (23: 25: 25: 27: 27) patt reps.

Cont in patt as now set for a further 8 rows.

Fasten off.

Join right shoulder and Neck Border seam.

Join side seams.

Armhole borders (both alike)

With RS facing and C/2 hook, rejoin yarn at top of one side seam, 1 ch (does NOT count as st), work 1 round of sc evenly around entire armhole edge, ending with sl st to first sc, turn.

Next round: (WS) 1 ch (does NOT count as st), 1 sc into each sc to end, sl st to first sc.

Fasten off.

Hem border

With RS facing and C/2 hook, rejoin yarn at base of one side seam, 1 ch (does NOT count as st), work 1 round of sc evenly around entire lower edge, ending with sl st to first sc, turn.

Next round: (WS) 1 ch (does NOT count as st), 1 sc into each sc to end, sl st to first sc.

Fasten off.

Combine textures and colors to create the simplest of shawls to keep you elegantly covered up and cozy. Don't let the fancy yarn put you off – the shawl is really easy to make and you'll have it finished in no time at all!

Mini Shawl

MEASUREMENTS

Actual size

15³/₄ × 53¹/₂ in

40 × 136 cm

MATERIALS

- 7 × 1³/₄ oz (50 g) balls of Lion Brand Fancy Fur in Tropical Turquoise 248
- N/15 (10.00 mm) crochet hook

GAUGE

8 sts and 4¹/₂ rows to 4 in (10 cm) measured over pattern using N/15 hook. Change hook size if necessary to obtain this gauge.

ABBREVIATIONS

See page 15.

BODY

With N/15 hook, ch 4.

Row 1: (RS) 1 dc into 4th ch from hook, turn. 2 sts.

Row 2: 3 ch (count as first dc), skip dc at base of 3 ch, 2 dc between dc just skipped and 3 ch at beg of previous row, turn. 3 sts.

Row 3: 3 ch (count as first dc), skip dc at base of 3 ch, 2 dc between dc just skipped and next dc, skip 1 dc, 1 dc between dc just skipped and 3 ch at beg of previous row, turn. 4 sts.

Row 4: 3 ch (count as first dc), skip dc at base of 3 ch and next dc, 2 dc between dc just skipped and next dc, skip 1 dc, 2 dc between dc just skipped and 3 ch at beg of previous row, turn. 5 sts.

Row 5: 3 ch (count as first dc), skip dc at base of 3 ch, 2 dc between dc just skipped and next dc, skip 2 dc, 2 dc between dc just skipped and next dc, skip 1 dc, 1 dc between dc just skipped and 3 ch at beg of previous row, turn. 6 sts.

Row 6: 3 ch (count as first dc), skip dc at base of 3 ch and next dc, 2 dc between dc just skipped and next dc, skip 2 dc, 2 dc between dc just skipped and next dc, skip 1 dc, 2 dc between dc just skipped and 3 ch at beg of previous row, turn. 7 sts.

Row 7: 3 ch (count as first dc), skip dc at base of 3 ch, 2 dc between dc just skipped and next dc, [skip 2 dc, 2 dc between dc just skipped and next dc] twice, skip 1 dc, 1 dc between dc just skipped and 3 ch at beg of previous row, turn. 8 sts.

Row 8: 3 ch (count as first dc), skip dc at base of 3 ch and next dc, 2 dc between dc just skipped and next dc, [skip 2 dc, 2 dc between dc just skipped and next dc] twice, skip 1 dc, 2 dc between dc just skipped and 3 ch at beg of previous row, turn. 9 sts.

Row 9: 3 ch (count as first dc), skip dc at base of 3 ch, 2 dc between dc just skipped and next

dc, [skip 2 dc, 2 dc between dc just skipped and next dc] 3 times, skip 1 dc, 1 dc between dc just skipped and 3 ch at beg of previous row, turn. 10 sts.

Row 10: 3 ch (count as first dc), skip dc at base of 3 ch and next dc, 2 dc between dc just skipped and next dc, [skip 2 dc, 2 dc between dc just skipped and next dc] 3 times, skip 1 dc, 2 dc between dc just skipped and 3 ch at beg of previous row, turn. 11 sts.

Row 11: 3 ch (count as first dc), skip dc at base of 3 ch, 2 dc between dc just skipped and next dc, [skip 2 dc, 2 dc between dc just skipped and next dc] 4 times, skip 1 dc, 1 dc between dc just skipped and 3 ch at beg of previous row, turn. 12 sts.

Row 12: 3 ch (count as first dc), skip dc at base of 3 ch and next dc, 2 dc between dc just skipped and next dc, [skip 2 dc, 2 dc between dc just skipped and next dc] 4 times, skip 1 dc, 2 dc between dc just skipped and 3 ch at beg of previous row, turn. 13 sts.

Row 13: 3 ch (count as first dc), skip dc at base of 3 ch, 2 dc between dc just skipped and next dc, [skip 2 dc, 2 dc between dc just skipped and next dc] 5 times, skip 1 dc, 1 dc between dc just skipped and 3 ch at beg of previous row, turn. 14 sts.

Row 14: 3 ch (count as first dc), skip dc at base of 3 ch and next dc, 2 dc between dc just skipped and next dc, [skip 2 dc, 2 dc between dc just skipped and next dc] 5 times, skip 1 dc, 2 dc between dc just skipped and 3 ch at beg of previous row, turn. 15 sts. Cont in this way,

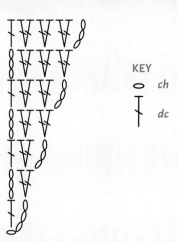

KEY

o ch

⊤ dc

■ Ironing a yarn like this one would spoil the texture
of it. So, once your shawl is complete, simply shake
it out to raise the pile, and wear it!

■ This little shawl will look just as good worn around
your shoulders, forming a cozy "collar," as it will if
you tie it loosely around on your hips and wear it
as a big sash-style belt.

working 1 more dc on every row as now set,
until following row has been worked:

Row 31: 3 ch (count as first dc), skip dc at base of
3 ch, 2 dc between dc just skipped and next dc,
[skip 2 dc, 2 dc between dc just skipped and next
dc] 14 times, skip 1 dc, 1 dc between dc just skipped and 3 ch at beg of previous row, turn. 32 sts.

Row 32: 3 ch (count as first dc), skip dc at base
of 3 ch and next dc, 2 dc between dc just
skipped and next dc, [skip 2 dc, 2 dc between
dc just skipped and next dc] 14 times, turn,
leaving last 2 dc unworked. 31 sts.

Row 33: 3 ch (count as first dc), skip dc at base
of 3 ch and next 2 dc, 2 dc between dc just
skipped and next dc, [skip 2 dc, 2 dc between
dc just skipped and next dc] 13 times, skip 1 dc,
1 dc between dc just skipped and 3 ch at beg of
previous row, turn. 30 sts.

Row 34: 3 ch (count as first dc), skip dc at base
of 3 ch and next dc, 2 dc between dc just
skipped and next dc, [skip 2 dc, 2 dc between
dc just skipped and next dc] 13 times, turn,
leaving last 2 dc unworked. 29 sts.

Row 35: 3 ch (count as first dc), skip dc at base
of 3 ch and next 2 dc, 2 dc between dc just
skipped and next dc, [skip 2 dc, 2 dc between
dc just skipped and next dc] 12 times, skip 1 dc,
1 dc between dc just skipped and 3 ch at beg of
previous row, turn. 28 sts.

Row 36: 3 ch (count as first dc), skip dc at base
of 3 ch and next dc, 2 dc between dc just
skipped and next dc, [skip 2 dc, 2 dc between
dc just skipped and next dc] 12 times, turn,

leaving last 2 dc unworked. 27 sts.

Row 37: 3 ch (count as first dc), skip dc at base
of 3 ch and next 2 dc, 2 dc between dc just
skipped and next dc, [skip 2 dc, 2 dc between
dc just skipped and next dc] 11 times, skip 1 dc,
1 dc between dc just skipped and 3 ch at beg of
previous row, turn. 26 sts.

Row 38: 3 ch (count as first dc), skip dc at base
of 3 ch and next dc, 2 dc between dc just
skipped and next dc, [skip 2 dc, 2 dc between
dc just skipped and next dc] 11 times, turn,
leaving last 2 dc unworked. 25 sts. Cont in this
way, working 1 less dc on every row as now set,
until the following row has been worked:

Row 58: 3 ch (count as first dc), skip dc at base of
3 ch and next dc, 2 dc between dc just skipped
and next dc, skip 2 dc, 2 dc between dc just skipped and next dc, turn, leaving last 2 dc
unworked. 5 sts.

Row 59: 3 ch (count as first dc), skip dc at base of
3 ch and next 2 dc, 2 dc between dc just skipped
and next dc, skip 1 dc, 1 dc between dc just skipped and 3 ch at beg of previous row, turn. 4 sts.

Row 60: 3 ch (count as first dc), skip dc at base
of 3 ch and next dc, 2 dc between dc just skipped and next dc, turn, leaving last 2 dc
unworked. 3 sts.

Row 61: 3 ch (count as first dc), skip dc at base of
3 ch and next dc, 1 dc between dc just skipped
and 3 ch at beg of previous row. 2 sts. Fasten off.

FINISHING

Do NOT iron.

Tubes of bead-encrusted single crochet are all you need to make this stunning jewelry. Make your necklace as long or as short as you like, and choose beads to match your outfit. Or why not make a whole wardrobe of bracelets and necklaces?

Bracelet and Necklace

 INTERMEDIATE

MEASUREMENTS

BRACELET

Circumference
7³/₄ in
20 cm

NECKLACE

Length when fastened
16¹/₂ in
42 cm

MATERIALS

Bracelet and Necklace
- 2 × 1³/₄ oz (50 g) balls of Lion Brand Glitterspun in Ruby 113
- C/2 (2.50 mm) crochet hook
- Approx 1,200 beads
- 1 button for Necklace

GAUGE

26 sts and 30 rows to 10 cm (4 in) measured over beaded single crochet fabric using C/2 hook. Change hook size if necessary to obtain this gauge.

ABBREVIATIONS

See page 15.
For how to work with beads, see pages 16–17.

BRACELET

Thread beads onto yarn. With C/2 hook, ch 6 and join with a sl st to form a ring
Foundation round: (WS) 1 ch (does NOT count as st), 1 sc into each ch to end.
Cont in patt as follows:
Round 1: (WS) 1 beaded sc into each sc to end.
Round 2: (WS) 1 beaded sc into each beaded sc to end. Round 2 forms patt.**
Cont in spiraling rounds of beaded sc until strip is approx 7³/₄ in (20 cm) long – check this length is long enough that, when the ends are joined, bracelet will fit over hand.
Fasten off.

FINISHING

Do NOT iron. Join ends of strip.

NECKLACE

Work as given for Bracelet to **.
Cont in spiraling rounds of beaded sc until strip is 42 cm (16¹/₂ in) long.
Now work buttonloop as follows: 7 beaded ch, sl st to opposite side of last round. Fasten off.

FINISHING

Do NOT iron. Sew ends of strip closed, making sure buttonloop is left free. Attach button to other end of strip.

KEY
o   ch
•   sl st
+   sc
⊕   beaded sc

■ Mix together lots of different-colored beads and make
  your bracelet or necklace multicolored. It's a great
  way to use up beads left over from other projects!
■ When making the bracelet, make sure the strip is long
  enough to be able to slide your hand through before
  fastening off. Measure around your hand, at the
  widest point, and adjust the length of the strip if
  necessary. But remember – it will stretch slightly
  as you put it on.

Combine glittering Lurex® yarn and sparkling beads to create this pull-on hat and matching skinny scarf. Made in a simple lacy stitch, the edges are finished with a scallop edging – and all sprinkled with beads!

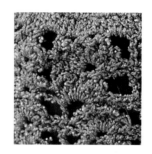

Skinny Scarf and Hat

INTERMEDIATE ★★☆

MEASUREMENTS

SCARF

Actual size
5 × 95¹/₂ in
13 × 243 cm

HAT

Width around head
17¹/₄ in
44 cm

MATERIALS

- 8 × 1³/₄ oz (50 g) balls of Lion Brand Glitterspun in Sapphire 109
- C/2 (2.50 mm) crochet hook
- Approx 2,500 beads

GAUGE

3 pattern repeats (30 sts) measure 3³/₄ in (9.5 cm) and 12 rows to 4 in (10 cm) measured over pattern using C/2 hook. Change hook size if necessary to obtain this gauge.

ABBREVIATIONS

sc2tog – *insert hook as indicated, yo and draw loop through, rep from * once more, yo and draw through all 3 loops on hook; **dc2tog** – *yo and insert hook as indicated, yo and draw loop through, yo and draw through 2 loops, rep from * once more, yo and draw through all 3 loops on hook.
See also page 15.

For how to work with beads, see pages 16–17.

SCARF

Thread beads onto yarn.
With C/2 hook, ch 32.
Foundation row: (WS) 1 sc into 2nd ch from hook, *3 ch, skip 3 ch, 1 sc into next ch, 3 ch, skip 1 ch, 1 sc into next ch, 3 ch, skip 3 ch, 1 sc into next ch, rep from * to end, turn.
3 patt reps.
Next row: 1 ch (does NOT count as st), 1 sc into first sc, *1 ch, skip (3 ch and 1 sc), dc2tog into next ch sp, [1 ch, 1 beaded ch, 1 ch and dc2tog] 4 times into same ch sp, 1 ch, skip (1 sc and 3 ch), 1 sc into next sc, rep from * to end, turn.
Cont in patt as follows:
Row 1: (WS) 7 ch (count as first tr and 3 ch), skip (sc at base of 7 ch, 1 ch, dc2tog, 1 ch, 1 beaded ch, 1 ch and dc2tog), *1 sc into next ch sp working sc after beaded ch, 3 ch, skip dc2tog, 1 sc into next ch sp working sc before beaded ch, 3 ch, skip (dc2tog, 1 ch, 1 beaded ch, 1 ch, dc2tog and 1 ch), 1 tr into next sc**, 3 ch, (skip (1 ch, dc2tog, 1 ch, 1 beaded ch, 1 ch and

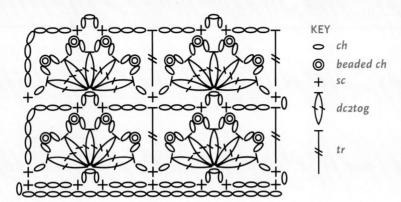

KEY
○ ch
◎ beaded ch
+ sc
⟨⟩ dc2tog
⊤ tr

dc2tog), rep from * to end, ending last rep at **, turn.

Row 2: 1 ch (does NOT count as st), 1 sc into first tr, *1 ch, skip (3 ch and 1 sc), dc2tog into next ch sp, [1 ch, 1 beaded ch, 1 ch and dc2tog] 4 times into same ch sp, 1 ch, skip (1 sc and 3 ch), 1 sc into next tr, rep from * to end, working sc at end of last rep into 4th of 7 ch at beg of previous row, turn.

These 2 rows form patt.

Cont in patt until scarf measures approx 94^{1}/$_{2}$ in (240 cm), ending with patt row 2 and a RS row.

Next row: (WS) 7 ch (count as first tr and 3 ch), skip (sc at base of 7 ch, 1 ch, dc2tog, 1 ch, 1 beaded ch, 1 ch and dc2tog), *1 sc into next ch sp working sc after beaded ch, 1 ch, skip dc2tog, 1 sc into next ch sp working sc before beaded ch, 3 ch, skip (dc2tog, 1 ch, 1 beaded ch, 1 ch, dc2tog and 1 ch), 1 tr into next sc**, 3 ch, (skip (1 ch, dc2tog, 1 ch, 1 beaded ch, 1 ch and dc2tog), rep from * to end, ending last rep at **, turn.

Do NOT fasten off.

Edging

Thread beads onto yarn.

With RS facing, work around entire outer edge of scarf as follows: 1 ch (does NOT count as st), work across top of last row as follows: 1 sc into tr at end of last row and mark this sc, [3 sc into next ch sp, 1 sc into next sc, 1 sc into next ch sp, 1 sc into next sc, 3 sc into next ch

sp] 3 times, 1 sc into 4th of 7 ch at beg of previous row and mark this sc, work down first row-end edge in sc, working a multiple of 6 sc plus 3 sc, 1 sc into foundation ch at base of first sc of foundation row and mark this sc, [3 sc into next ch sp, 1 sc into next ch at base of a sc of foundation row, 1 sc into next ch sp, 1 sc into next ch at base of a sc of foundation row, 3 sc into next ch sp] 3 times, 1 sc into ch at base of last sc of foundation row and mark this sc, work up other row-end edge in sc, working a multiple of 6 sc plus 3 sc, sl st to first marked sc.

Next round: (RS) 1 ch (does NOT count as st), 1 sc into same place as sl st at end of previous round – this is first marked corner sc, skip 1 sc, *(3 dc, 1 ch, 1 beaded ch, 1 ch, sl st to top of last dc, and 3 dc) into next sc**, skip 2 sc, 1 sc into next sc, skip 2 sc, rep from * to end, noting that either side of marked corner sc only 1 sc will be skipped (so that sc of this round is worked into corner sc and next dc group is only 1 st away from corner sc) and ending last rep at **, skip last sc, sl st to first sc. Fasten off.

FINISHING

Iron very carefully following instructions on yarn label, taking care not to damage the beads.

■ *This scarf and hat combines a Lurex® yarn and matching color silver-lined beads but you could use contrasting or multicolored beads to give a completely different look.*

■ *Why not try wearing the scarf round your waist as a wide sash-style belt? This would jazz up a plain pair of pants or a skirt and, if the belt loops are wide enough, you could easily thread it through them.*

HAT

Thread beads onto yarn.

With C/2 hook, ch 140 and join with a sl st to form a ring.

Round 1: (WS) 1 ch (does NOT count as st), 1 sc into first ch, *3 ch, skip 3 ch, 1 sc into next ch, 3 ch, skip 1 ch, 1 sc into next ch, 3 ch, skip 3 ch, 1 sc into next ch, rep from * to end, replacing sc at end of last rep with sl st to first sc, **turn.** 14 patt reps.

Round 2: 1 ch (does NOT count as st), 1 sc into first sc, *1 ch, skip (3 ch and 1 sc), dc2tog into next ch sp, [1 ch, 1 beaded ch, 1 ch and dc2tog] 4 times into same ch sp, 1 ch, skip (1 sc and 3 ch), 1 sc into next sc, rep from * to end, replacing sc at end of last rep with sl st to first sc, turn.

Round 3: 7 ch (count as first tr and 3 ch), skip (sc at base of 7 ch, 1ch, dc2tog, 1 ch, 1 beaded ch, 1 ch and dc2tog), *1 sc into next ch sp working sc after beaded ch, 3 ch, skip dc2tog, 1 sc into next ch sp working sc before beaded ch, 3 ch, skip (dc2tog, 1 ch, 1 beaded ch, 1 ch, dc2tog and 1 ch)**, 1 tr into next sc, 3 ch, (skip (1 ch, dc2tog, 1 ch, 1 beaded ch and dc2tog), rep from * to end, ending last rep at **, sl st to 4th of 7 ch at beg of round, turn.

Round 4: 1 ch (does NOT count as st), 1 sc into same place as sl st at end of previous round, *1 ch, skip (3 ch and 1 sc), dc2tog into next ch sp, [1 ch, 1 beaded ch, 1 ch and dc2tog] 4 times into same ch sp, 1 ch, skip (1 sc and 3 ch), 1 sc into next tr, rep from * to end, replacing sc at end of last rep with sl st to first sc, turn.

Rounds 5 to 12: As rounds 3 and 4.

Round 13: 7 ch (count as first tr and 3 ch), skip (sc at base of 7 ch, 1 ch, dc2tog, 1 ch, 1 beaded ch, 1 ch and dc2tog), *1 sc into next ch sp working sc after beaded ch, 1 ch, skip dc2tog, 1 sc into next ch sp working sc before beaded ch, 3 ch, skip (dc2tog, 1 ch, 1 beaded ch, 1 ch, dc2tog and 1 ch)**, 1 tr into next sc, 3 ch, (skip (1 ch, dc2tog, 1 ch, 1 beaded ch, 1 ch and dc2tog), rep from * to end, ending last rep at **, sl st to 4th of 7 ch at beg of round, turn.

Round 14: (RS) 3 ch (count as first dc), skip st at base of 3 ch, *3 dc into next ch sp, 1 dc into next sc, 1 dc into next ch sp, 1 dc into next sc, 3 dc into next ch sp**, 1 dc into next tr, rep from * to end, ending last rep at **, sl st to top of 3 ch at beg of round, do NOT turn. 140 sts. Without turning at ends of rounds (so that all foll rounds are RS rounds) cont as follows with unbeaded yarn:

Round 15: 3 ch (count as first dc), skip st at base of 3 ch, 1 dc into each of next 7 dc, [dc2tog over next 2 dc, 1 dc into each of next 8 dc] 13 times, dc2tog over last 2 dc, sl st to top of 3 ch at beg of round. 126 sts.

Round 16: 3 ch (count as first dc), skip st at base of 3 ch, 1 dc into each of next 6 dc, [dc2tog over next 2 sts, 1 dc into each of next 7 dc] 13 times, dc2tog over last 2 sts, sl st to top of 3 ch at beg of round. 112 sts.

Round 17: 3 ch (count as first dc), skip st at base of 3 ch, 1 dc into each of next 5 dc, [dc2tog over next 2 sts, 1 dc into each of next 6 dc] 13 times, dc2tog over last 2 sts, sl st to top of 3 ch at beg of round. 98 sts.

Round 18: 3 ch (count as first dc), skip st at base of 3 ch, 1 dc into each of next 4 dc, [dc2tog over next 2 sts, 1 dc into each of next 5 dc] 13 times, dc2tog over last 2 sts, sl st to top of 3 ch at beg of round. 84 sts.

Round 19: 3 ch (count as first dc), skip st at base of 3 ch, 1 dc into each of next 3 dc, [dc2tog over next 2 sts, 1 dc into each of next 4 dc] 13 times, dc2tog over last 2 sts, sl st to top of 3 ch at beg of round. 70 sts.

Round 20: 3 ch (count as first dc), skip st at base of 3 ch, 1 dc into each of next 2 dc, [dc2tog over next 2 sts, 1 dc into each of next 3 dc] 13 times, dc2tog over last 2 sts, sl st to top of 3 ch at beg of round. 56 sts.

Round 21: 3 ch (count as first dc), skip st at base of 3 ch, 1 dc into next dc, [dc2tog over next 2 sts, 1 dc into each of next 2 dc] 13 times, dc2tog over last 2 sts, sl st to top of 3 ch at beg of round. 42 sts.

Round 22: 3 ch (count as first dc), skip st at base of 3 ch, [dc2tog over next 2 sts, 1 dc into next dc] 13 times, dc2tog over last 2 sts, sl st to top of 3 ch at beg of round. 28 sts.

Round 23: 3 ch (do NOT count as st), skip st at base of 3 ch, 1 dc into next st, [dc2tog over next 2 sts] 13 times, sl st to top of first dc of round. 14 sts.

Round 24: 1 ch (does NOT count as st), [sc2tog over next 2 sts] 7 times, sl st to first sc2tog, for top trim now ch 11, 1 sc into 2nd ch from hook, 1 sc into each of next 9 ch.
Fasten off.

FINISHING
Iron very carefully following instructions on yarn label, taking care not to damage the beads.
Run a gathering thread around top of last round and pull up tight. Fasten off securely, catching free end of top trim inside center.

Edging
Thread beads onto yarn.
With RS facing and using C/2 hook, rejoin yarn to foundation ch edge of Hat, 1 ch (does NOT count as st), work 126 sc evenly around entire foundation ch edge (this is 9 sc for each rep), sl st to first sc.
Next round: (RS) 1 ch (does NOT count as st), 1 sc into same place as sl st at end of previous round, *skip 2 sc, (3 dc, 1 ch, 1 beaded ch, 1 ch, sl st to top of last dc, and 3 dc) into next sc, skip 2 sc, 1 sc into next sc, rep from * to end, replacing sc at end of last rep with sl st to first sc.
Fasten off.

Basic single crochet fabric in a twinkling Lurex® yarn is encrusted with beads to create the opulent look of these accessories. Use big faceted beads or mix metallic, faceted and glass beads of all shapes and sizes to make the belt.

Cuff Bracelet and Sash Belt

EASY

MEASUREMENTS

CUFF BRACELET
Actual size
$2^1/_4 \times 6^3/_4$ in
6×17 cm

SASH BELT
Actual size (excluding fringe)
$2^1/_4 \times 49^1/_4$ in
6×125 cm

MATERIALS
Cuff Bracelet
- $1 \times 1^3/_4$ oz (50 g) ball of Lion Brand Glitterspun in Onyx 153
- C/2 (2.50 mm) crochet hook
- 163 faceted crystal beads
- 4 buttons

Sash belt
- $4 \times 1^3/_4$ oz (50 g) balls of Lion Brand Glitterspun in Bronze 135
- C/2 (2.50 mm) crochet hook
- Approx 1,600 mixed beads

GAUGE
26 sts and 30 rows to 4 in (10 cm) measured over beaded double crochet fabric using C/2 hook. Change hook size if necessary to obtain this gauge.

ABBREVIATIONS
See page 15.

For how to work with beads, see pages 16–17.

CUFF BRACELET
Thread beads onto yarn.
With C/2 hook, ch 16.
Foundation row: (RS) 1 sc into 2nd ch from hook, 1 sc into each ch to end, turn. 15 sc.
Cont in patt as follows:
Row 1: (WS) 1 ch (does NOT count as st), 1 sc into first sc, *1 beaded sc into next sc, 1 sc into next sc, rep from * to end, turn.
Row 2: 1 ch (does NOT count as st), 1 sc into each sc to end, turn.
Row 3: 1 ch (does NOT count as st), 1 sc into first sc, *1 sc into next sc, 1 beaded sc into next sc, rep from * to last 2 sc, 1 sc into each of last 2 sc, turn.
Row 4: As row 2.
These 4 rows form patt.
Cont in patt for a further 46 rows, ending after patt row 2 and with a RS row.
Do NOT turn at end of last row.

Edging
Next round: (RS) 1 ch (does NOT count as st), work in sc evenly down row-end edge, across

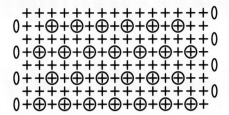

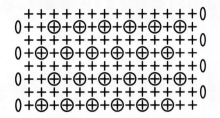

KEY

○ *ch*

+ *sc*

⊕ *beaded sc*

foundation ch edge, and up other row-end edge to beg of last row, 1 sc into first sc of last row of main piece, [3 ch (to make a buttonloop), skip 2 sc, 1 sc into each of next 2 sc] 3 times, 3 ch, skip 2 sc, sl st to sc at beg of round.

Fasten off.

Attach buttons to correspond with buttonloops.

SASH BELT

Thread beads onto yarn.

With C/2 hook, ch 15.

Foundation row: (RS) 1 sc into 2nd ch from hook, 1 sc into each ch to end, turn. 14 sc.

Cont in patt as follows:

Row 1: (WS) 1 ch (does NOT count as st), 1 sc into first sc, *1 beaded sc into next sc, 1 sc into next sc, rep from * to last sc, 1 sc into last sc, turn.

Row 2: 1 ch (does NOT count as st), 1 sc into each sc to end, turn.

Row 3: 1 ch (does NOT count as st), 1 sc into first sc, *1 sc into next sc, 1 beaded sc into next sc, rep from * to last sc, 1 sc into last sc, turn.

Row 4: As row 2.

These 4 rows form patt.

Cont in patt until Sash Belt measures 49¼ in (125 cm), ending with a RS row.

Fasten off.

Edging

With RS facing and using C/2 hook, rejoin yarn to foundation ch at end of first row, 1 ch (does NOT count as st), now work 1 row of crab st (sc worked from left to right, instead of right to left) along one row-end edge to end of last row of main section, turn, with WS facing work across 14 sts of last row as follows: 1 sc into first sc, [31 ch, 1 sc into 2nd ch from hook, 1 sc into each of next 29 ch, 1 sc into each of next 4 sc of last row] 3 times, 31 ch, 1 sc into 2nd ch from hook, 1 sc into each of next 29 ch, 1 sc into last sc of last row, turn, now work 1 row of crab st (sc worked from left to right, instead of right to left) along other row-end edge to end of first row of main section, turn, with WS facing work across 14 sts of foundation ch edge as follows: 1 sc into first st, [31 ch, 1 sc into 2nd ch from hook, 1 sc into each of next 29 ch, 1 sc into each of next 4 sts of foundation ch edge] 3 times, 31 ch, 1 sc into 2nd ch from hook, 1 sc into each of next 29 ch, 1 sc into last st of foundation ch edge, sl st to first sc.

Fasten off.

■ *This belt uses lots of different sorts of beads, from tiny metallic gold beads to quite large teardrop-faceted glass beads. Mix together all the beads before you start and thread them onto the yarn randomly.*

■ *When making the bracelet, make sure the strip is long enough to fit around your wrist and adjust the length if you need to. But remember that it will stretch a little in wear.*

Wondrously simple to make, using just double crochet, this big wrap is sure to get you noticed! Worked in an exquisite rainbow ribbon yarn, combining every color imaginable, it's bound to match any and every outfit in your wardrobe.

Wrap

 EASY

MEASUREMENTS

Actual size, excluding fringe
37¹/₂ × 78 in
95 × 198 cm

MATERIALS

- 16 × 1³/₄ oz (50 g) balls of Lion Brand Incredible in Purple Party 207
- N/15 (10.00 mm) crochet hook

GAUGE

8 sts and 4 rows to 4 in (10 cm) measured over double crochet fabric using N/15 hook. Change hook size if necessary to obtain this gauge.

ABBREVIATIONS

See page 15.

KEY
o ch
T dc

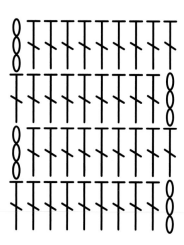

BODY

With N/15 hook, ch 78.
Row 1: (RS) 1 dc into 4th ch from hook, 1 dc into each ch to end, turn. 76 sts.
Row 2: 3 ch (count as first dc), skip dc at base of 3 ch, 1 dc into each dc to end, working last dc into top of 3 ch at beg of previous row, turn.
Last row forms dc fabric.
Cont in dc fabric until Wrap measures 78 in (198 cm).
Fasten off.

FINISHING

Do NOT iron.
Cut 23¹/₂ in (60 cm) lengths of yarn and knot one length through each st along foundation ch edge and along top of last row to form fringe.

- *There's no need to iron your wrap once it's completed as this would spoil the full, rounded look of the stitches. But if the strands that make up the fringe become a little crumpled, simply mist them lightly with a water spray and let them hang free to dry naturally. This should remove any creases that may have formed.*
- *If you feel the very long fringe may be a bit too much for you, simply make it shorter. Or you could try knotting a few fancy beads onto some of the strands of the fringe to make it even more special.*
- *The amazing colors of this ribbon yarn turn simple double crochet into something really special!*

Take a simple mesh-stitch tank top, add a glittering Lurex®
yarn and a generous sprinkling of glittery beads for this little
tank top. At home with jeans or at the grandest of parties,
the top works up in little time.

Beaded Tank Top

MEASUREMENTS

To fit bust

32	34	36	38	40	42	in
81	86	91	97	102	107	cm

Actual size, at underarm

33¹/₂	35	37¹/₄	39	41¹/₄	43	in
85	89	95	99	105	109	cm

Actual length

19³/₄	20	20¹/₂	20³/₄	21¹/₄	21¹/₂	in
50	51	52	53	54	55	cm

MATERIALS

- 6 (8: 8: 10: 12) × 1³/₄ oz (50 g) balls of Lion Brand Glitterspun in Sapphire 109
- C/2 (2.50 mm) crochet hook
- Approx 9,160 (9,810: 10,650: 11,340: 12,220: 12,960) beads

GAUGE

28 sts and 14 rows to 4 in (10 cm) measured over pattern using C/2 hook. Change hook size if necessary to obtain this gauge.

ABBREVIATIONS

dc2tog – *yo and insert hook as indicated, yo and draw loop through, yo and draw through 2 loops, rep from * once more, yo and draw through all 3 loops on hook.
See also page 15.

For how to work with beads, see pages 15–16.

BACK AND FRONT (both alike)

Thread beads onto yarn. With C/2 hook, ch 116 (122: 130: 136: 144: 150) and 1 beaded ch - ch 117 (123: 131: 137: 145: 151) in total.

Row 1: (RS) 1 dc into 5th ch from hook, *1 beaded ch, skip 1 ch, 1 dc into next ch, rep from * to end, turn. 115 (121: 129: 135: 143: 149) sts, 57 (60: 64: 67: 71: 74) beaded ch sps. Cont in patt as follows:

Row 2: 3 ch (count as first dc), skip dc at end of previous row, *1 beaded ch, skip 1 beaded ch, 1 dc into next dc, rep from * to end, working last dc into top of 3 ch at beg of previous row, turn. This row forms patt.

Work in patt for 1 row more.

Row 4: (WS) 3 ch (do NOT count as st), skip (1 dc and 1 beaded ch) at end of last row, 1 dc into next dc – 1 beaded ch sp decreased, patt to last 3 sts, dc2tog over last 3 sts, working first "leg" into next dc, skipping beaded ch, and working 2nd "leg" into top of 3 ch at beg of previous row – 1 beaded ch sp decreased, turn.

Working all decreases as set by last row, dec 1 beaded ch sp at each end of 3rd and every foll 3rd row until 49 (52: 56: 59: 63: 66) beaded ch sps rem.

Work 7 rows more.

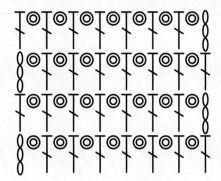

Row 21: 3 ch (count as first dc), 1 beaded ch, 1 dc into dc at end of previous row – 1 beaded ch sp increased, patt until dc has been worked into top of 3 ch at beg of previous row, 1 beaded ch, 1 dc into same place as last dc – 1 beaded ch sp increased, turn.
Working all increases as set by last row, inc 1 beaded ch sp at each end of 4th and every foll 4th row until there are 59 (62: 66: 69: 73: 76) beaded ch sps.
Cont even until work measures 11^1/$_2$ (11^3/$_4$: 11^3/$_4$: 12^1/$_4$: 12^1/$_4$: 12^1/$_2$) in, 29 (30: 30: 31: 31: 32) cm.

Shape armholes

Next row: sl st across first 6 (8: 8: 10: 10: 12) sts and into next dc, 3 ch (do NOT count as st), skip 1 beaded ch, 1 dc into next dc – 4 (5: 5: 6: 6: 7) beaded ch sps decreased, work in patt to last 9 (11: 11: 13: 13: 15) sts, dc2tog over next 3 sts, working first "leg" into next dc, skipping beaded ch, and working 2nd "leg" into next dc and turn, leaving rem 6 (8: 8: 10: 10: 12) sts unworked – 4 (5: 5: 6: 6: 7) beaded ch sps decreased. 51 (52: 56: 57: 61: 62) beaded ch sps.
Working all decreases in same way as for side seam decreases, dec 1 beaded ch sp at each end of next 7 (7: 8: 8: 9: 9) rows. 75 (77: 81: 83: 87: 89) sts, 37 (38: 40: 41: 43: 44) beaded ch sps.

Shape neck

Next row: patt until 10th (10th: 11th: 11th: 12th: 12th) beaded ch has been worked, dc2tog over next 3 sts, working first "leg" into next dc, skipping beaded ch, and working 2nd "leg" into next dc and turn, leaving rem sts unworked. 10 (10: 11: 11: 12: 12) beaded ch sps.
**Working all decreases in same way as for side seam decreases, dec 1 beaded ch sp at neck edge of next 7 rows. 7 (7: 9: 9: 11: 11) sts, 3 (3: 4: 4: 5: 5) beaded ch sps.
Cont even until armhole measures 7^3/$_4$ (7^3/$_4$: 8^1/$_4$: 8^1/$_4$: 8^1/$_2$: 8^1/$_2$) in, 20 (20: 21: 21: 22: 22) cm.
Fasten off.
Return to last complete row worked, skip center 29 (31: 31: 33: 33: 35) sts, rejoin yarn to next dc and cont as follows:
Next row: 3 ch (do NOT count as st), skip st where yarn was rejoined and next beaded ch, 1 dc into next dc, patt to end, turn. 10 (10: 11: 11: 12: 12) beaded ch sps.
Complete to match first side from **.

FINISHING

Iron very carefully following instructions on yarn label, taking care not to damage the beads.
Join shoulder seams. Join side seams.

- *Wear this little tank top over a camisole if you feel it's a little too revealing on its own!*
- *When working the beaded chains that make up this mesh pattern, ensure that the beads always fall underneath the chain stitch so that all the beads show on the right side of the work.*
- *Make sure you check your gauge over the beaded mesh pattern using the beads you intend to use for the actual garment, as the size of the beads affects the gauge.*

- *This top uses so many beads, it is quite heavy when it's completed! If you want to simplify it, why not try leaving the beads off either the edging or the mesh pattern? Do this by simply replacing each beaded stitch with a plain stitch.*
- *The weight of the beads on this little top makes it best to store the garment flat, rather than on a hanger. If you leave it hanging up, the weight of the beads will pull it down and stretch it out of shape, and you could end up with a long, thin vest!*

Hem Edging

With RS facing and using C/2 hook, rejoin yarn at base of one side seam, 1 ch (does NOT count as st), work one round of sc evenly around entire lower edge, ending with sl st to first sc, turn.

Round 1: (WS) 1 ch (does NOT count as st), 1 beaded sc into each sc to end, sl st to first beaded sc, turn.

Round 2: 1 ch (does NOT count as st), 1 sc into each beaded sc to end, sl st to first sc, turn.

Round 3: As round 1.

Fasten off.

Neck and Armhole Edgings

Work to match hem edging, rejoining yarn at a seam and skipping sc as required while working round 2 to ensure Edging lies flat.

GLITTER

Shimmer and glitter in these sparkling designs, all worked in fine Lurex® yarns. The metallic shades of gold, pewter, bronze, copper and silver yarn give you all the glitter you may need – but, if you want more, why not choose one of the designs with sequins and beads? They are guaranteed to make you a twinkling star on that big night.

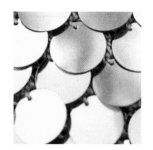

The big, bold gold sequins on this simple halter neck top, worked in a smooth and silky yarn, make it a style to really get you noticed. Not one for shrinking violets!

Sequin Halter Neck

INTERMEDIATE

MEASUREMENTS

To fit bust

32	34	36	38	40	42	in
81	86	91	97	102	107	cm

Actual size, at underarm

32	34	36	37³/₄	39³/₄	41³/₄	in
81	86	91	96	101	106	cm

Actual length, from underarm

12¹/₄	12¹/₂	12¹/₂	13	13	13¹/₄	in
31	32	32	33	33	34	cm

MATERIALS

- 10 (10: 12: 14: 14: 16) × 1³/₄ oz (50 g) balls of Crystal Palace Crème 2001 in Ivory
- B/1 (2.00 mm) crochet hook
- Approx 2,300 (2,500: 2,600: 2,900: 3,000: 3,300) large gold sequins

GAUGE

32 sts and 20 rows to 4 in (10 cm) measured over pattern using B/1 hook. Change hook size if necessary to obtain this gauge.

ABBREVIATIONS

sc2tog – *insert hook as indicated, yo and draw loop through, rep from * once more, yo and draw through all 3 loops on hook; **sc3tog** – *insert hook as indicated, yo and draw loop through, rep from * twice more, yo and draw through all 4 loops on hook; **dc2tog** – *yo and insert hook as indicated, yo and draw loop through, yo and draw through 2 loops, rep from * once more, yo and draw through all 3 loops on hook; **dc3tog** – *yo and insert hook as indicated, yo and draw loop through, yo and draw through 2 loops, rep from * twice more, yo and draw through all 4 loops on hook. *See also page 15.*

For how to work with sequins, see page 16–17.

BACK

Thread sequins onto yarn.

With B/1 hook, ch 118 (126: 134: 142: 150: 158).

Row 1: (RS) 1 sc into 2nd ch from hook, 1 sc into each ch to end, turn. 117 (125: 133: 141: 149: 157) sts.

Row 2: 1 ch (does NOT count as st), 1 sc into each sc to end, turn.

Rows 3 and 4: As row 2.

Cont in patt as follows:

Row 1: (RS) 3 ch (count as first dc), skip sc at base of 3 ch, 1 dc into each sc to end, turn.

Row 2: 1 ch (does NOT count as st), 1 sc into each of first 2 dc, *1 sequinned sc into next dc, 1 sc into each of next 3 dc, rep from * to

■ Make sure the sequins have the hole near one edge, not in the center, or they will not lie flat.
■ Twilleys Silky is a very slippery yarn and the stitches can easily fall undone. Each time you put your work down, it's a good idea to slip the working loop onto a safety pin to make sure it does not unravel!
■ This garment is designed to skim over the body and the actual finished size is about the same as the size it is to fit. If you want a tighter-fitting garment, make a smaller size.
■ When working the top edge shaping, remember not to place any sequins on the actual edge stitches of the rows as these edge sequins will get in the way when working the edgings.
■ The sequins will tend to fold themselves out of position as this top is made. Once finished and in wear, gently smooth them all downward to create the shimmery fish-scale effect.

last 3 sts, 1 sequinned sc into next dc, 1 sc into each of last 2 sts, working last sc into top of 3 ch at beg of previous row, turn.

Row 3: As row 1.

Row 4: 1 ch (does NOT count as st), 1 sc into each of first 4 dc, *1 sequinned sc into next dc, 1 sc into each of next 3 dc, rep from * to last 5 sts, 1 sequinned sc into next dc, 1 sc into each of last 4 sts, working last sc into top of 3 ch at beg of previous row, turn.

These 4 rows form patt.

Cont in patt for a further 2 rows, ending with a WS row.

Dec row: (RS) 3 ch (count as first dc), skip sc at base of 3 ch, dc2tog over next 2 sc – 1 st decreased, 1 dc into each sc to last 3 sc, dc2tog over next 2 sc – 1 st decreased, 1 dc into last sc, turn.

Working all decreases as set by last row, dec 1 st at each end of every foll 4th row until 109 (117: 125: 133: 141: 149) sts rem.

Work 3 rows, ending with a WS row.

Inc row: (RS) 3 ch (count as first dc), skip sc at base of 3 ch, 2 dc into next sc – 1 st increased, 1 dc into each sc to last 2 sc, 2 dc into next sc – 1 st increased, 1 dc into last sc, turn.

Working all increases as set by last row, inc 1 st at each end of every foll 4th row until there are 129 (137: 145: 153: 161: 169) sts, taking inc sts into patt.

Work a further 1 (3: 3: 5: 5: 7) rows, ending with a WS row.**

Fasten off.

FRONT

Work as given for Back to **.

Shape armholes

Next row: (RS) sl st across and into 7th (9th: 11th: 13th: 15th: 17th) st, 3 ch (count as first dc), skip sc at base of 3 ch, 1 dc into each sc to last 6 (8: 10: 12: 14: 16) sc and turn, leaving rem sts unworked. 117 (121: 125: 129: 133: 137) sts.

Next row: 1 ch (does NOT count as st), sc2tog over first 2 dc – 1 st decreased, patt to last 2 sts, sc2tog over last 2 sts – 1 st decreased, turn. 115 (119: 123: 127: 131: 135) sts.

Working all decreases as set by last row and Back side seam shaping, dec 1 st at each end of next 2 rows, ending with a WS row. 111 (115: 119: 123: 127: 131) sts.

Shape neck

Next row: (RS) 3 ch (count as first dc), skip sc at base of 3 ch, dc2tog over next 2 sc – 1 st decreased, 1 dc into each of next 48 (50: 52: 54: 56: 58) sc, dc3tog over next 3 sc – 2 sts decreased, 1 dc into next sc and turn, leaving rem sts unworked. 52 (54: 56: 58: 60: 62) sts.

Next row: 1 ch (does NOT count as st), sc3tog over first 3 sts – 2 sts decreased, patt to last 2 sts, sc2tog over last 2 sts – 1 st decreased, turn. 49 (51: 53: 55: 57: 59) sts.

Working all decreases as now set, dec 2 sts at neck edge and 1 st at armhole edge of next 15 (15: 16: 17: 17: 18) rows, ending with a RS (RS: WS: RS: RS: WS) row. 4 (6: 5: 4: 6: 5) sts.

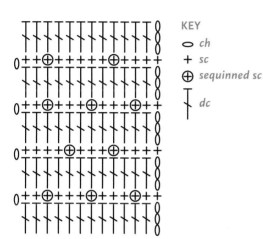

KEY

o   *ch*
+   *sc*
⊕   *sequinned sc*
†   *dc*

For 1st, 2nd, 4th and 5th sizes

Next row: (WS) 1 ch (does NOT count as st),
[sc2tog over next 2 sts] 2 (o: 2: o) times,
[sc3tog over next 3 sts] o (2: o: 2) times. 2 sts.

For 3rd and 4th sizes

Next row: (RS) 3 ch (do NOT count as st),
dc3tog over next 3 sts, 1 dc into last sc. 2 sts.

All sizes

Fasten off.
Return to last complete row worked, skip
center sc, rejoin yarn to next sc with RS
facing, 3 ch (count as first dc), skip sc at base
of 3 ch, dc3tog over next 3 sc – 2 sts decreased,
1 dc into each sc to last 3 sc, dc2tog over next
2 sc – 1 st decreased, 1 dc into last sc, turn. 52
(54: 56: 58: 60: 62) sts. Complete to match
first side, reversing shaping.

FINISHING

Do NOT iron.
Join side seams.

Front neck border

With RS facing and B/1 hook, rejoin yarn at
left front fasten-off point, 1 ch (does NOT
count as st), work in sc down left front slope,
then up right front slope to right front fasten-
off point, working sc2tog either side of base of
V neck, turn.
Next row: 1 ch (does NOT count as st), 1 sc into
each sc to end, working sc2tog either side of
base of V neck, turn.
Rep last row twice more.
Fasten off.

Back and armhole borders and ties

With B/1 hook, ch 150, with RS facing and
starting at top of Front Neck Border, work
in sc evenly down right front armhole edge,
across top of Back, then up left front armhole
edge to top of other end of Front Neck Border,
151 ch, turn.
Next row: (WS) 1 sc into 2nd ch from hook,
1 sc into each ch and sc to end, turn.
Next row: 1 ch (does NOT count as st), 1 sc into
each sc to end, turn.
Rep last row once more.
Fasten off.

Top off a simple dress with this neat bolero. Worked in a simple crunchy textured stitch, the edges are outlined with a row of bright and shiny sequins.

Bolero

INTERMEDIATE

MEASUREMENTS

To fit bust

32	34	36	38	40	42	in
81	86	91	97	102	107	cm

Actual size, at underarm

$33^3/_4$	$35^3/_4$	38	$39^3/_4$	$41^3/_4$	44	in
86	91	97	101	106	112	cm

Actual length

$13^1/_4$	$13^3/_4$	14	$14^1/_2$	15	$15^1/_4$	in
34	35	36	37	38	39	cm

Actual sleeve

$17^3/_4$	18	18	$18^1/_2$	$18^1/_2$	$18^1/_2$	in
45	46	46	47	47	47	cm

MATERIALS

- 14 (16: 18: 20: 22: 24) × $1^3/_4$ oz (50 g) balls of Lion Brand Glitterspun in Silver 150
- C/2 (2.50 mm) crochet hook
- Approx 350 (370: 390: 400: 420: 430) large silver sequins

GAUGE

32 sts and 20 rows to 4 in (10 cm) measured over pattern using C/2 hook. Change hook size if necessary to obtain this gauge.

ABBREVIATIONS

hdc2tog – *yo and insert hook as indicated, yo and draw loop through, rep from * once more, yo and draw through all 5 loops on hook;
hdc3tog – *yo and insert hook as indicated, yo and draw loop through, rep from * twice more, yo and draw through all 7 loops on hook.
See also page 15.

For how to work with sequins, see pages 16–17.

BACK

With C/2 hook, ch 120 (129: 138: 144: 153: 162).
Foundation row: (RS) (1 sc, 1 ch and 1 dc) into 3rd ch from hook, *skip 2 ch, (1 sc, 1 ch and 1 dc) into next ch, rep from * to last 3 ch, skip 2 ch, 1 hdc into last ch, turn. 119 (128: 137: 143: 152: 161) sts, 39 (42: 45: 47: 50: 53) patt reps.
Cont in patt as follows:
Row 1: 2 ch (count as first hdc), skip first hdc and next dc, *(1 sc, 1 ch and 1 dc) into next ch sp**, skip (1 sc and 1 dc), rep from * to end, ending last rep at **, skip 1 sc, 1 hdc into top of turning ch, turn.
This row forms patt.
Keeping patt correct, cont as follows:
Work 2 rows, ending with a WS row.
Next row: (RS) 2 ch (count as first hdc), 1 hdc

- *The crunchy texture of the simple stitch pattern used for this bolero contrasts well with the sleek shine of the sequins.*
- *Make sure you iron the bolero pieces before you work the sequined edging. Once the sequins are attached, you cannot iron them, as even a warm iron could melt them. If you need to iron your completed bolero, take great care to cover the sequins with a cloth or simply block it out to shape.*
- *When working the sequined edging, you may find it easier to thread all the sequins onto one skein of yarn. Use a plain skein for the first and last round of the edging, and the skein with the sequins for the sequined round. This will save repeatedly having to slide all the sequins along the yarn to work the plain rounds.*
- *This bolero has large sequins that match the yarn color – but you could use contrasting-colored sequins, smaller ones or even fancy beads.*

into hdc at base of 2 ch – 1 st increased, skip next dc, *(1 sc, 1 ch and 1 dc) into next ch sp**, skip (1 sc and 1 dc), rep from * to end, ending last rep at **, skip 1 sc, 2 hdc into top of turning ch – 1 st increased, turn.

Next row: 2 ch (count as first hdc), 1 hdc into hdc at base of 2 ch, 1 ch – 2 sts increased, 1 hdc into next hdc, skip next 1 dc, *(1 sc, 1 ch and 1 dc) into next ch sp**, skip (1 sc and 1 dc), rep from * to end, ending last rep at **, skip 1 sc, 1 hdc into next hdc, 1 ch, 2 hdc into top of turning ch – 2 sts increased, turn. 125 (134: 143: 149: 158: 167) sts.

Work in patt 1 row across all sts, working first and last patt rep into ch sp between hdc. 41 (44: 47: 49: 52: 55) patt reps. (1 patt rep increased at each edge over 3 rows.)

Working all increases as now set, cont as follows: Work 2 rows.

Inc 1 patt rep at each edge over next 3 rows. Rep last 5 rows once more. 137 (146: 155: 161: 170: 179) sts, 45 (48: 51: 53: 56: 59) patt reps. Cont even until back measures 4³/₄ (5: 5: 5¹/₂: 5¹/₂: 6) in, 12 (13: 13: 14: 14: 15) cm, ending with a WS row.

Shape armholes

Next row: (RS) sl st across first 6 sts and into 7th st, 2 ch (count as first hdc) – 2 patt reps decreased, work in patt to last 7 sts, 1 hdc into next st and turn, leaving rem 6 sts unworked - 2 patt reps decreased. 125 (134: 143: 149: 158: 167) sts, 41 (44: 47: 49: 52: 55) patt reps.

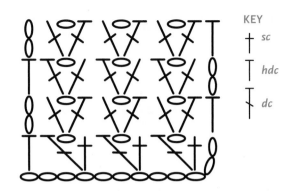

Next row: 2 ch (do NOT count as st), hdc2tog over next 2 sts, 1 hdc into next st – 2 sts decreased, patt to last 5 sts, skip next sc, 1 hdc into next dc, hdc3tog over next 3 sts – 2 sts decreased, turn.

Next row: 2 ch (do NOT count as st), 1 hdc into next st – 1 st decreased, patt to last 2 sts, hdc2tog over next hdc and hdc2tog – 1 st decreased. 119 (128: 137: 143: 152: 161) sts.

Work in patt 1 row across all sts. 39 (42: 45: 47: 50: 53) patt reps. (1 patt rep decreased at each edge over 3 rows.)

Rep last 3 rows 2 (3: 4: 5: 6: 6) times more. 107 (110: 113: 113: 116: 125) sts, 35 (36: 37: 37: 38: 41) patt reps.

Cont even until armholes measure 7³/₄ (7³/₄: 8¹/₄: 8¹/₄: 8¹/₂: 8¹/₂) in, 20 (20: 21: 21: 22: 22) cm, ending with a WS row.

Fasten off, placing markers either side of center 55 (58: 61: 61: 64: 61) sts to denote back neck.

LEFT FRONT

With C/2 hook, ch 60 (63: 69: 72: 75: 81).

Work foundation row as given for back. 59 (62: 68: 71: 74: 80) sts, 19 (20: 22: 23: 24: 26) patt reps.

Cont in patt as given for back as follows:

Work 3 rows, ending with a WS row.

Working all shaping as given for back, cont as follows:

Inc 1 patt rep at side seam edge of next 3 rows.

Work 2 rows.

Rep last 5 rows once more, then first 3 rows

again. 68 (71: 77: 80: 83: 89) sts, 22 (23: 25: 26: 27: 29) patt reps.

Cont even until left front matches back to start of armhole shaping, ending with a WS row.

Shape armhole

Dec 6 sts, 2 patt reps at beg of next row. 62 (65: 71: 74: 77: 83) sts, 20 (21: 23: 24: 25: 27) patt reps.

Shape front slope

Dec 1 patt rep at armhole and at front slope edge over next 3 rows, 3 (4: 5: 6: 7: 7) times. 44 (41: 41: 38: 35: 41) sts, 14 (13: 13: 12: 11: 13) patt reps.

Work 1 row, then dec 1 patt rep at front slope edge over next 3 rows.

Rep last 4 rows 5 (4: 4: 3: 2: 2) times more. 26 (26: 26: 26: 26: 32) sts, 8 (8: 8: 8: 8: 10) patt reps.

Cont straight until left front matches back to shoulder, ending with a WS row.

Fasten off.

RIGHT FRONT

Work to match left front, reversing shapings.

SLEEVES

With C/2 hook, ch 78 (78: 81: 81: 84: 84).

Work foundation row as given for back. 77 (77: 80: 80: 83: 83) sts, 25 (25: 26: 26: 27: 27) patt reps.

Cont in patt as given for back as follows:

Work 7 rows, ending with a WS row.

Working all shaping as given for back, cont as follows:

Inc 1 patt rep at each end over next 3 rows.

Work 13 (13: 13: 13: 11: 11) rows.

Rep last 16 (16: 16: 16: 14: 14) rows 3 (3: 3: 3: 4: 4) times more, then first 3 of these rows again. 107 (107: 110: 110: 119: 119) sts, 35 (35: 36: 36: 39: 39) patt reps.

Cont even until sleeve measures 17 ($17^1/4$: $17^1/4$: $17^3/4$: $17^3/4$: $17^3/4$) in, 43 (44: 44: 45: 45: 45) cm, ending with a RS row.

Shape top

Working all shaping as given for back, dec 6 sts, 2 patt reps at each end of next row. 95 (95: 98: 98: 107: 107) sts, 31 (31: 32: 32: 35: 35) patt reps.

Dec 1 patt rep at each end over next 3 rows,

8 (8: 8: 8: 9: 9) times. 47 (47: 50: 50: 53: 53) sts, 15 (15: 16: 16: 17: 17) patt reps.

Fasten off.

FINISHING

Iron carefully following instructions on yarn label.

Join shoulder seams. Join side seams. Join sleeve seams. Sew sleeves into armholes.

Edging

Thread sequins onto yarn.

With C/2 hook, rejoin yarn at base of one side seam, 1 ch (does NOT count as st), work 1 round of sc evenly around entire hem, front opening and neck edges, ending with sl st to first sc and ensuring an even number of sts are worked, turn.

Next round: (WS) 1 ch (does NOT count as st), *1 sc into next sc, 1 sequinned sc into next sc, rep from * to end, sl st to first sc, turn.

Next round: 1 ch (does NOT count as st), 1 sc into each st to end, sl st to first sc.

Fasten off.

Work edging around lower edge of sleeves in same way, rejoining yarn at base of sleeve seam.

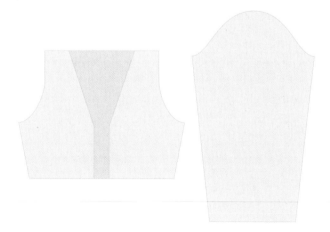

Combining metallic shades of silver, bronze and gold, this loose fitting top is made up of lots of clever motifs. The motifs are joined as they are made, so there's no sewing up afterward.

Kimono Top

INTERMEDIATE

MEASUREMENTS

One size, to fit bust
34–42 in
86–107 cm

Actual size
47¹/₄ in
120 cm

Actual length
11³/₄ in
30 cm

Actual sleeve
11³/₄ in
30 cm

MATERIALS

- 4 × 1³/₄ oz (50 g) balls of Lion Brand Glitterspun in Silver 150; 4 × 1³/₄ oz (50 g) balls of Lion Brand Glitterspun Gold 170; 6 × 1³/₄ oz (50 g) balls of Lion Brand Glitterspun in Bronze 135
- C/2 (2.50 mm) crochet hook

GAUGE

Motif measures 4 in (10 cm) square on C/2 hook. Change hook size if necessary to obtain this gauge.

ABBREVIATIONS

picot – 3 ch, sl st to top of sc just worked; **dtr** - double treble.
See also page 15.

MOTIF

With C/2 hook and first color (either A or B), ch 4 and join with a sl st to form a ring.

Round 1: (RS) 1 ch (does NOT count as st), 1 sc into ring, [4 ch, 1 dtr into ring, 4 ch, 1 sc into ring] 4 times, replacing sc at end of last rep with sl st to first sc.
Break off first color and join in second color (either B or A) to same place as sl st.

Round 2: 11 ch (count as first tr and 7 ch), skip (first sc and 4 ch), *1 sc into next dtr, 7 ch**, skip 4 ch, 1 dc into next sc, 7 ch, skip 4 ch, rep from * to end, ending last rep at **, sl st to 4th of 11 ch at beg of round.

Round 3: 4 ch (count as first tr), 2 dc into st at base of 4 ch, *1 ch, 1 sc into next ch sp, 1 ch, (3 dtr, 2 ch and 3 dtr) into next sc, 1 ch, 1 sc into next ch sp, 1 ch**, 3 tr into next tr, rep from * to end, ending last rep at **, sl st to top of 4 ch at beg of round.

Round 4: 1 ch (does NOT count as st), 1 sc into same place as sl st at end of previous round, 1 sc into each of next 2 tr, *1 sc into next ch sp, 1 sc into next sc, 1 sc into next ch sp, 1 sc into each of next 2 dtr, skip next dtr, 3 sc into next ch sp, skip next dtr, 1 sc into each of next 2 dtr, 1 sc into next ch sp, 1 sc into next sc, 1 sc into next ch sp**, 1 sc into each of next 3 tr, rep from * to end, ending last rep at **, sl st to first sc. 64 sts.
Break off second color and join in C to 2nd sc at beg of round.

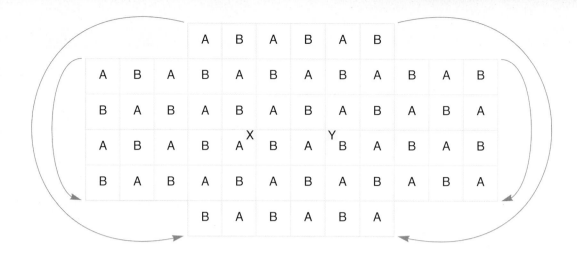

				A	B	A	B	A	B				
A	B	A	B	A	B	A	B	A	B	A	B	
B	A	B	A	B	A	B	A	B	A	B	A	
A	B	A	B	A^X	B	A^Y	B	A	B	A	B	
B	A	B	A	B	A	B	A	B	A	B	A	
				B	A	B	A	B	A			

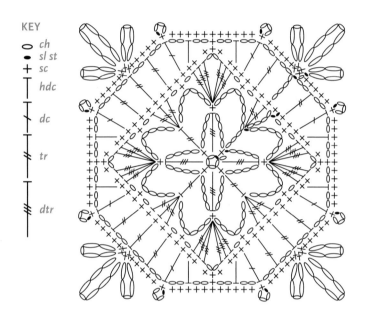

KEY

○ ch
● sl st
+ sc
┬ hdc
╁ dc
╪ tr
╪╪ dtr

Round 5: 6 ch (count as first tr and 2 ch), skip 1 sc, 1 tr into next sc, *2 ch, skip 1 sc, 1 dc into next sc, 2 ch, skip 1 sc, 1 hdc into next sc, 2 ch, skip 1 sc, 1 sc into next sc, 2 ch, skip 1 sc, 1 hdc into next sc, 2 ch, skip 1 sc, 1 dc into next sc**, [2 ch, skip 1 sc, 1 tr into next sc] 3 times, rep from * to end, ending last rep at **, 2 ch, skip 1 sc, 1 tr into next sc, 2 ch, skip 1 sc, sl st to 4th of 6 ch at beg of round.

Round 6: 1 ch (does NOT count as st), (1 sc, 5 ch, 1 sc, 7 ch, 1 sc, 5 ch and 1 sc) into same place as sl st at end of previous round, *2 sc into next ch sp, 1 sc into next tr, 2 sc into next ch sp, 1 sc into next dc, 1 picot, [2 sc into next ch sp, 1 sc into next st] 4 times, 1 picot, 2 sc into next ch sp, 1 sc into next tr, 2 sc into next

ch sp**, (1 sc, 5 ch, 1 sc, 7 ch, 1 sc, 5 ch and 1 sc) into next tr, rep from * to end, ending last rep at **, sl st to first sc. Fasten off.

Motif should be 4 in (10 cm) square – adjust hook size now if required.

In all corners of motif, there are three ch loops – a central 7-ch loop with a 5-ch loop each side, and along sides of motif between these groups of ch loops there are 2 picots of 3 ch. While working Round 6, join motifs at corners, by replacing corner (7 ch) with (3 ch, 1 sl st into corner 7-ch loop of adjacent motif, 3 ch), and at picots, by replacing picot (3 ch) with (1 ch, 1 sl st into picot of adjacent motif, 1 ch).

TOP

Following diagram, make and join 60 motifs to form shape shown. On diagram, letter indicates color to use for round 1 – either A or B. If using A for round 1, use B for rounds 2 to 4, and vice versa. Use C for rounds 5 and 6 of **ALL** motifs. Join side and underarm seams while joining motifs as indicated by arrows, and do NOT join motifs between X and Y to form neck opening (join first "shoulder" motifs at the picots but NOT at the corners nearest the neck edge).

FINISHING

Iron carefully following instructions on yarn label.

Encrusted with faceted beads, this stylish cardigan will make sure you sparkle! Worked in a combination of single and double crochet, it's the stunning beads that give this design its impact.

Beaded Cardigan

ADVANCED ★★★

MEASUREMENTS

To fit bust

32	34	36	38	40	42	in
81	86	91	97	102	107	cm

Actual size, at underarm

$34^1/_4$	$36^1/_4$	$37^3/_4$	$39^3/_4$	$41^1/_4$	$43^1/_4$ in
87	92	96	101	105	110	cm

Actual length

$22^1/_2$	$22^3/_4$	$23^1/_4$	$23^1/_2$	24	$24^1/_4$ in
57	58	59	60	61	62	cm

Actual sleeve

$17^3/_4$	$17^3/_4$	18	18	18	$18^1/_2$ in
45	45	46	46	46	47	cm

MATERIALS

- 24 (25: 26: 28: 29: 30) × $3^1/_2$ oz (100 g) balls of Rowan Lurex® Shimmer in Copper 330
- C/2 (2.50 mm) crochet hook
- Approx 1,800 (1,900: 2,000: 2,100: 2,200: 2,300) × crystal beads
- 5 buttons

GAUGE

26 sts and 18 rows to 4 in (10 cm) measured over pattern using C/2 hook. Change hook size if necessary to obtain this gauge.

ABBREVIATIONS

sc2tog – *insert hook as indicated, yo and draw loop through, rep from * once more, yo and draw through all 3 loops on hook; **dc2tog** – *yo and insert hook as indicated, yo and draw loop through, yo and draw through 2 loops, rep from * once more, yo and draw through all 3 loops on hook.
See also page 15.

For how to work with beads, see pages 16–17.

BACK

Thread 200 beads onto yarn.
With C/2 hook, ch 111 (117: 123: 129: 135: 141).
Foundation row: (RS) 1 dc into 4th ch from hook, 1 dc into each ch to end, turn. 109 (115: 121: 127: 133: 139) sts.
Cont in patt as follows:
Row 1: (WS) 1 ch (does NOT count as st), 1 sc into each of first 6 (3: 6: 3: 6: 3) dc, 1 beaded sc into next dc, *1 sc into each of next 5 dc, 1 beaded sc into next dc, rep from * to last 6 (3: 6: 3: 6: 3) sts, 1 sc into each of last 6 (3: 6: 3: 6: 3) sts, working last sc into top of 3 ch at beg of previous row, turn.
Row 2: 3 ch (count as first dc), skip sc at base of 3 ch, 1 dc into each sc to end, turn.

■ *Rowan Lurex® Shimmer is quite a delicate yarn and could be easily damaged by repeatedly slipping too many beads along it. To avoid the risk of this happening, thread the beads onto the yarn in batches of about 200 beads. Then, break the yarn and thread on some more.*

■ *When working the shaping, don't place a bead on an edge stitch of a row as this will make it difficult to sew up the seam.*

Row 3: 1 ch (does NOT count as st), 1 sc into each dc to end, working last sc into top of 3 ch at beg of previous row, turn.

Row 4: As row 2.

Row 5: 1 ch (does NOT count as st), 1 sc into each of first 3 (6: 3: 6: 3: 6) dc, 1 beaded sc into next dc, *1 sc into each of next 5 dc, 1 beaded sc into next dc, rep from * to last 3 (6: 3: 6: 3: 6) sts, 1 sc into each of last 3 (6: 3: 6: 3: 6) sts, working last sc into top of 3 ch at beg of previous row, turn.

Rows 6 and 7: As rows 2 and 3.

Row 8: 3 ch (do NOT count as st), skip sc at base of 3 ch, 1 dc into next sc – 1 st decreased, 1 dc into each sc to last 2 sc, dc2tog over last 2 sc – 1 st decreased, turn. 107 (113: 119: 125: 131: 137) sts.

These 8 rows form patt and start side seam shaping.

Keeping patt correct, cont as follows:

Work 2 rows, ending with a RS row.

Next row: (WS) 1 ch (does NOT count as st), sc2tog over first 2 dc – 1 st decreased, work in patt to last 2 sts, sc2tog over last 2 sts (second of these is the 3 ch at beg of previous row) – 1 st decreased, turn. 105 (111: 117: 123: 129: 135) sts.

Working all shaping as now set, dec 1 st at each end of 3rd and every foll 3rd row until 95 (101: 107: 113: 119: 125) sts rem.

Work 1 row, ending with a WS row.

Work mock belt

Row 1: (RS) 1 ch (does NOT count as st), working into back loops only of previous row, 1 sc into each sc to end, turn.

Row 2: 1 ch (does NOT count as st), 1 sc into each sc to end, turn.

Row 3: 1 ch (does NOT count as st), 1 sc into each sc to end, turn.

Row 4: (WS) 1 ch (does NOT count as st), 1 sc into each of first 2 sc, *1 beaded sc into next sc, 1 sc into each of next 2 sc, rep from * to end, turn.

Rows 5 to 10: As rows 3 and 4, 3 times.

Rows 11 to 13: As row 2.

Row 14: 1 ch (does NOT count as st), working into front loops only of previous row, 1 sc into each sc to end, turn.

These 14 rows complete mock belt.

Now cont in patt as follows:

Next row: (RS) 3 ch (count as first dc), 1 dc into sc at base of 3 ch – 1 st increased, 1 dc into each sc to last sc, 2 dc into last sc – 1 st increased, turn. 97 (103: 109: 115: 121: 127) sts.

Next row: 1 ch (does NOT count as st), 1 sc into each of first 6 (3: 6: 3: 6: 3) dc, 1 beaded sc into next dc, *1 sc into each of next 5 dc, 1 beaded sc into next dc, rep from * to last 6 (3: 6: 3: 6: 3) sts, 1 sc into each of last 6 (3: 6: 3: 6: 3) sts, working last sc into top of 3 ch at beg of previous row, turn.

Next row: 3 ch (count as first dc), skip sc at base of 3 ch, 1 dc into each sc to end, turn.

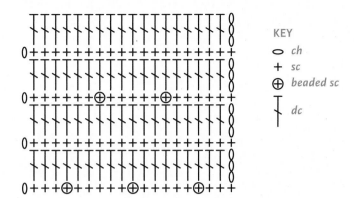

Next row: 1 ch (does NOT count as st), 2 sc into first dc – 1 st increased, 1 sc into each dc to last st, 2 sc into top of 3 ch at beg of previous row – 1 st increased, turn. 99 (105: 111: 117: 123: 129) sts.

Last 4 rows set position of patt and increases. Keeping patt correct as now set and working all increases as now set, inc 1 st at each end of every foll 3rd row until there are 113 (119: 125: 131: 137: 143) sts, taking inc sts into patt.

Cont even until back measures 14^{1}/$_{2}$ (15: 15: 15^{1}/$_{4}$: 15^{1}/$_{4}$: 15^{3}/$_{4}$) in, 37 (38: 38: 39: 39: 40) cm, ending with a RS row.

Shape armholes

Next row: (WS) sl st across first 4 (5: 5: 6: 6: 7) dc and into next dc, 1 ch (does NOT count as st), 1 sc into same dc as last sl st - 4 (5: 5: 6: 6: 7) sts decreased, work in patt to last 4 (5: 5: 6: 6: 7) sts and turn, leaving rem 4 (5: 5: 6: 6: 7) sts unworked - 4 (5: 5: 6: 6: 7) sts decreased. 105 (109: 115: 119: 125: 129) sts.

Working all decreases in same way as for side seam decreases, dec 1 st at each end of next 9 (10: 12: 13: 15: 16) rows. 87 (89: 91: 93: 95: 97) sts. Cont even until armholes measure 7^{3}/$_{4}$ (7^{3}/$_{4}$: 8^{1}/$_{4}$: 8^{1}/$_{4}$: 8^{1}/$_{2}$: 8^{1}/$_{2}$) in, 20 (20: 21: 21: 22: 22) cm, ending with a WS row.

Fasten off, placing markers either side of center 39 (41: 41: 43: 43: 43) sts to denote back neck.

LEFT FRONT

With C/2 hook, ch 61 (64: 67: 70: 73: 76.

Foundation row: (RS) 1 dc into 4th ch from hook, 1 dc into each ch to end, turn. 59 (62: 65: 68: 71: 74) sts. Cont in patt as follows:

Row 1: (WS) 1 ch (does NOT count as st), 1 sc into each of first 4 dc, 1 beaded sc into next dc, *1 sc into each of next 5 dc, 1 beaded sc into next dc, rep from * to last 6 (3: 6: 3: 6: 3) sts, 1 sc into each of last 6 (3: 6: 3: 6: 3) sts, working last sc into top of 3 ch at beg of previous row, turn.

Row 2: 3 ch (count as first dc), skip sc at base of 3 ch, 1 dc into each sc to end, turn.

Row 3: 1 ch (does NOT count as st), 1 sc into each dc to end, working last sc into top of 3 ch at beg of previous row, turn.

Row 4: As row 2.

Row 5: 1 ch (does NOT count as st), 1 sc into first dc, 1 beaded sc into next dc, *1 sc into each of next 5 dc, 1 beaded sc into next dc, rep from * to last 3 (6: 3: 6: 3: 6) sts, 1 sc into each of last 3 (6: 3: 6: 3: 6) sts, working last sc into top of 3 ch at beg of previous row, turn.

Rows 6 and 7: As rows 2 and 3.

Row 8: 3 ch (do NOT count as st), skip sc at base of 3 ch, 1 dc into next sc – 1 st decreased, 1 dc into each sc to end, turn. 58 (61: 64: 67: 70: 73) sts.

These 8 rows form patt and start side seam shaping.

Keeping patt correct, cont as follows:
Working all shaping as set by back, dec 1 st at side seam edge of every foll 3rd row until

- *If the last row of the back is a beaded row, omit the beads on the last row of each front so that you don't end up with two rows of beads colliding along the shoulder seams.*
- *This cardigan uses quite large faceted crystal beads – but you could use multicolored tiny beads to create a totally different look. Or you could leave the beads out entirely by simply replacing each beaded sc with an ordinary sc.*

52 (55: 58: 61: 64: 67) sts rem.
Work 1 row, ending with a WS row.

Work mock belt
Row 1: (RS) 1 ch (does NOT count as st), working into back loops only of previous row, 1 sc into each sc to end, turn.
Row 2: 1 ch (does NOT count as st), 1 sc into each sc to end, turn.
Row 3: 1 ch (does NOT count as st), 1 sc into each sc to end, turn.
Row 4: (WS) 1 ch (does NOT count as st), 1 sc into first sc, *1 beaded sc into next sc, 1 sc into each of next 2 sc, rep from * to end, turn.
Rows 5 to 10: As rows 3 and 4, 3 times.
Rows 11 to 13: As row 2.
Row 14: 1 ch (does NOT count as st), working into front loops only of previous row, 1 sc into each sc to end, turn.
These 14 rows complete mock belt.
Now cont in patt as follows:
Next row: (RS) 3 ch (count as first dc), 1 dc into sc at base of 3 ch – 1 st increased, 1 dc into each sc to end, turn. 53 (56: 59: 62: 65: 68) sts.
Next row: 1 ch (does NOT count as st), 1 sc into each of first 4 dc, 1 beaded sc into next dc, *1 sc into each of next 5 dc, 1 beaded sc into next dc, rep from * to last 6 (3: 6: 3: 6: 3) sts, 1 sc into each of last 6 (3: 6: 3: 6: 3) sts, working last sc into top of 3 ch at beg of previous row, turn.
Next row: 3 ch (count as first dc), skip sc at base of 3 ch, 1 dc into each sc to end, turn.
Next row: 1 ch (does NOT count as st), 1 sc into

each dc to last st, 2 sc into top of 3 ch at beg of previous row – 1 st increased, turn. 54 (57: 60: 63: 66: 69) sts.
Last 4 rows set position of patt and increases. Keeping patt correct as now set and working all increases as now set, inc 1 st at side seam edge of every foll 3rd row until there are 61 (64: 67: 70: 73: 76) sts, taking inc sts into patt. Cont even until left front matches back to start of armhole shaping, ending with a RS row.

Shape armhole
Working all shaping in same way as given for Back, dec 4 (5: 5: 6: 6: 7) sts at end of next row. 57 (59: 62: 64: 67: 69) sts.
Dec 1 st at armhole edge of next 9 (10: 12: 13: 15: 16) rows. 48 (49: 50: 51: 52: 53) sts.
Cont even until 14 (14: 14: 16: 16: 16) rows less have been worked than on back to shoulder fasten-off, ending with a WS row.

Shape neck
Next row: (RS) 3 ch (count as first dc), skip sc at base of 3 ch, 1 dc into each of next 34 (34: 35: 36: 37: 38) sc and turn, leaving rem 13 (14: 14: 14: 14: 14) sts unworked.
Dec 1 st at neck edge on next 10 rows, then on 1 (1: 1: 2: 2: 2) alt rows. 24 (24: 25: 25: 26: 27) sts.
Work 1 row, ending with a WS row.
Fasten off.
Mark positions for 5 buttons along Left Front opening edge – lowest button level with row 7 of mock belt, top button ³/₄ in, 2 cm, below

neck shaping, and rem 3 buttons evenly spaced between.

RIGHT FRONT

With C/2 hook, ch 61 (64: 67: 70: 73: 76).
Foundation row: (RS) 1 dc into 4th ch from hook, 1 dc into each ch to end, turn. 59 (62: 65: 68: 71: 74) sts.
Cont in patt as follows:
Row 1: (WS) 1 ch (does NOT count as st), 1 sc into each of first 6 (3: 6: 3: 6: 3) dc, 1 beaded sc into next dc, *1 sc into each of next 5 dc, 1 beaded sc into next dc, rep from * to last 4 sts, 1 sc into each of last 4 sts, working last sc into top of 3 ch at beg of previous row, turn.
Row 2: 3 ch (count as first dc), skip sc at base of 3 ch, 1 dc into each sc to end, turn.
Row 3: 1 ch (does NOT count as st), 1 sc into each dc to end, working last sc into top of 3 ch at beg of previous row, turn.
Row 4: As row 2.
Row 5: 1 ch (does NOT count as st), 1 sc into each of first 3 (6: 3: 6: 3: 6) dc, 1 beaded sc into next dc, *1 sc into each of next 5 dc, 1 beaded sc into next dc, rep from * to last st, 1 sc into top of 3 ch at beg of previous row, turn.
Rows 6 and 7: As rows 2 and 3.
Row 8: 3 ch (count as first dc), skip sc at base of 3 ch, 1 dc into each sc to last 2 sc, dc2tog over last 2 sc – 1 st decreased, turn. 58 (61: 64: 67: 70: 73) sts.
These 8 rows form patt and start side seam shaping.

Keeping patt correct, cont as follows:
Working all shaping as set by back, dec 1 st at side seam edge of 3rd and every foll 3rd row until 52 (55: 58: 61: 64: 67) sts rem.
Work 1 row, ending with a WS row.

Work mock belt
Row 1: (RS) 1 ch (does NOT count as st), working into back loops only of previous row, 1 sc into each sc to end, turn.
Row 2: 1 ch (does NOT count as st), 1 sc into each sc to end, turn.
Row 3: 1 ch (does NOT count as st), 1 sc into each sc to end, turn.
Row 4: (WS) 1 ch (does NOT count as st), 1 sc into each of first 2 sc, *1 beaded sc into next sc, 1 sc into each of next 2 sc, rep from * to last 2 sc, 1 beaded sc into next sc, 1 sc into last sc, turn.
Rows 5 and 6: As rows 3 and 4.
Row 7: 1 ch (does NOT count as st), 1 sc into each of first 3 sc, 2 ch, skip 2 sc (to make a buttonhole), 1 sc into each sc to end, turn.
Row 8: 1 ch (does NOT count as st), 1 sc into each of first 2 sc, *1 beaded sc into next sc, 1 sc into each of next 2 sc, rep from * to last 5 sts, 2 sc into next ch sp, 1 sc into next sc, 1 beaded sc into next sc, 1 sc into last sc, turn.
Rows 9 and 10: As rows 3 and 4.
Rows 11 to 13: As row 2.
Row 14: 1 ch (does NOT count as st), working into front loops only of previous row, 1 sc into each sc to end, turn.

These 14 rows complete mock belt.

Now cont in patt as follows:

Next row: (RS) 3 ch (count as first dc), skip sc at base of 3 ch, 1 dc into each sc to last sc, 2 dc into last sc – 1 st increased, turn. 53 (56: 59: 62: 65: 68) sts.

Next row: 1 ch (does NOT count as st), 1 sc into each of first 6 (3: 6: 3: 6: 3) dc, 1 beaded sc into next dc, *1 sc into each of next 5 dc, 1 beaded sc into next dc, rep from * to last 4 sts, 1 sc into each of last 4 sts, working last sc into top of 3 ch at beg of previous row, turn.

Next row: 3 ch (count as first dc), skip sc at base of 3 ch, 1 dc into each sc to end, turn.

Next row: 1 ch (does NOT count as st), 2 sc into first dc – 1 st increased, 1 sc into each dc to end, working last sc into top of 3 ch at beg of previous row, turn. 54 (57: 60: 63: 66: 69) sts.

Last 4 rows set position of patt and increases.

Complete to match left front, reversing shapings and working a further 4 buttonholes to correspond with positions marked for buttons as follows:

Buttonhole row: (WS) 1 ch (does NOT count as st), patt to last 5 sts, 2 ch, skip 2 dc (to make a buttonhole – on next row work 2 dc into this ch sp), patt rem 3 sts, turn.

SLEEVES

With C/2 hook, ch 58 (58: 60: 62: 62: 64).

Row 1: (RS) 1 sc into 2nd ch from hook, 1 sc into each ch to end, turn. 57 (57: 59: 61: 61: 63) sts.

Row 2: 1 ch (does NOT count as st), 1 sc into each sc to end, turn.

Row 3: 1 ch (does NOT count as st), 1 sc into each sc to end, turn.

Row 4: (WS) 1 ch (does NOT count as st), 1 sc into each of first 1 (1: 2: 3: 3: 1) sc, *1 beaded sc into next sc, 1 sc into each of next 2 sc, rep from * to last 2 (2: 3: 4: 4: 2) sc, 1 beaded sc into next sc, 1 sc into each of last 1 (1: 2: 3: 3: 1) sc, turn.

Rows 5 to 10: As rows 3 and 4, 3 times.

Rows 11 to 13: As row 2.

Row 14: 1 ch (does NOT count as st), working into front loops only of previous row, 1 sc into each sc to end, turn.

These 14 rows complete mock cuff.

Cont in patt as follows:

Row 1: (RS) 3 ch (count as first dc), 1 dc into sc at base of 3 ch – 1 st increased, 1 dc into each sc to last sc, 2 dc into last sc – 1 st increased, turn. 59 (59: 61: 63: 63: 65) sts.

Row 2: 1 ch (does NOT count as st), 1 sc into each of first 5 (5: 6: 1: 1: 2) dc, 1 beaded sc into next dc, *1 sc into each of next 5 dc, 1 beaded sc into next dc, rep from * to last 5 (5: 6: 1: 1: 2) sts, 1 sc into each of last 5 (5: 6: 1: 1: 2) sts, working last sc into top of 3 ch at beg of previous row, turn.

Row 3: 3 ch (count as first dc), skip sc at base of 3 ch, 1 dc into each sc to end, turn.

Row 4: 1 ch (does NOT count as st), 1 sc into each dc to end, working last sc into top of 3 ch at beg of previous row, turn.

Row 5: As row 1. 61 (61: 63: 65: 65: 67) sts.

Row 6: 1 ch (does NOT count as st), 1 sc into each of first 3 (3: 4: 5: 5: 6) dc, 1 beaded sc into

next dc, *1 sc into each of next 5 dc, 1 beaded sc into next dc, rep from * to last 3 (3: 4: 5: 5: 6) sts, 1 sc into each of last 3 (3: 4: 5: 5: 6) sts, working last sc into top of 3 ch at beg of previous row, turn.

Rows 7 and 8: As rows 3 and 4.

These 8 rows form patt and start sleeve shaping. Cont in patt, shaping sides by inc 1 st at each end of next and every foll 4th row to 67 (73: 75: 77: 83: 83) sts, then on every foll 6th row until there are 83 (85: 87: 89: 91: 93) sts, taking inc sts into patt.

Cont even until sleeve measures 17³/4 (17³/4: 18: 18: 18: 18¹/2) in, 45 (45: 46: 46: 46: 47) cm, ending with a RS row.

Shape top

Working all shaping as given for back, dec 4 (5: 5: 6: 6: 7) sts at each end of next row. 75 (75: 77: 77: 79: 79) sts.

Dec 1 st at each end of every row until 27 sts rem. Fasten off.

COLLAR

With RS facing and using C/2 hook, starting and ending on 5th sts in from front opening edges, work around neck edge as follows: 1 ch (does NOT count as st), 23 (23: 23: 25: 25: 25) sc up right side of neck, 38 (41: 41: 43: 43: 43) sc across back neck, then 23 (23: 23: 25: 25: 25) sc down left side of neck, turn. 84 (87: 87: 93: 93: 93) sts.

Row 1: (WS) 1 ch (does NOT count as st), 1 sc into first sc, 1 beaded sc into next sc, *1 sc into each of next 2 sc, 1 beaded sc into next sc, rep from * to last sc, 1 sc into last sc, turn.

Row 2: 1 ch (does NOT count as st), 1 sc into each of first 6 (7: 7: 8: 8: 8) sc, sc2tog over next 2 sc, *1 sc into each of next 12 (12: 12: 13: 13: 13) sc, sc2tog over next 2 sc, rep from * to last 6 (8: 8: 8: 8: 8) sc, 1 sc into each of last 6 (8: 8: 8: 8: 8) sc, turn. 78 (81: 81: 87: 87: 87) sts.

Row 3: As row 1.

Row 4: 1 ch (does NOT count as st), 1 sc into each of first 5 (4: 4: 5: 5: 5) sc, sc2tog over next 2 sc, *1 sc into each of next 11 (12: 12: 13: 13: 13) sc, sc2tog over next 2 sc, rep from * to last 6 (5: 5: 5: 5: 5) sc, 1 sc into each of last 6 (5: 5: 5: 5: 5) sc, turn. 72 (75: 75: 81: 81: 81) sts.

Row 5: As row 1.

Row 6: 1 ch (does NOT count as st), 1 sc into each of first 5 (4: 4: 4: 4: 4) sc, sc2tog over next 2 sc, *1 sc into each of next 10 (11: 11: 12: 12: 12) sc, sc2tog over next 2 sc, rep from * to last 5 (4: 4: 5: 5: 5) sc, 1 sc into each of last 5 (4: 4: 5: 5: 5) sc, turn. 66 (69: 69: 75: 75: 75) sts.

Row 7: As row 1.

Row 8: 1 ch (does NOT count as st), 1 sc into each sc to end, turn.

Row 9: As row 8.

Fasten off.

Join side seams. Join sleeve seams. Sew sleeves into armholes.

FINISHING

Do NOT iron.

Join shoulder seams.

Hem and lower front opening edging
With **WS** facing and C/2 hook, rejoin yarn to right front opening edge just below row 1 of mock belt, 1 ch (does NOT count as st), work 1 row of sc evenly down right front opening edge, across entire hem, then up left front opening edge to just below row 1 of mock belt, working 3 sc into hem corner points.
Fasten off.

Collar and upper front opening edging
With **WS** facing and C/2 hook, rejoin yarn to left front opening edge level with row 14 of mock belt, 1 ch (does NOT count as st), work 1 row of sc evenly up left front opening edge, around neck corner point and along to base of collar, working 3 sc into neck corner point, turn, work one row of crab st (sc worked from left to right, instead of right to left) around entire outer edge of collar, turn, work 1 row of sc evenly from base of collar across to right front opening edge, then down right front opening edge to level with row 14 of mock belt, working 3 sc into neck corner point.
Fasten off.

Mock belt edging
With **RS** facing and C/2 hook, rejoin yarn to left front opening edge level with row 14 of mock belt, 1 ch (does NOT count as st), working into rem free loops of row 13 of mock belt work 1 row of crab st (sc worked from left to right, instead of right to left) evenly around body to right front opening edge, then down right front opening edge of mock belt to loops left free by row 1 of mock belt, then work back around body working into this row of free loops to left front opening edge, then up left front opening edge to row 14 of mock belt.
Fasten off.

Upper mock cuff edging
With **RS** facing and C/2 hook, rejoin yarn to sleeve seam level with row 14 of mock cuff, 1 ch (does NOT count as st), working into rem free loops of row 13 of mock cuff work 1 round of crab st (sc worked from left to right, instead of right to left) evenly around sleeve, ending with sl st to first sc.
Fasten off.

Lower mock cuff edging
With **RS** facing and C/2 hook, rejoin yarn to base of sleeve seam, 1 ch (does NOT count as st), work 1 round of crab st (sc worked from left to right, instead of right to left) evenly around foundation ch edge, ending with sl st to first sc.
Fasten off.
Sew on buttons.

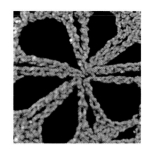

Simple triangular motifs make up this easy-to-wear skirt and wrap. A little time-consuming to make but worth the effort as you will want to wear them again and again. Team them with a little top or a cozy sweater – either way you'll sparkle.

Motif Skirt and Wrap

INTERMEDIATE

MEASUREMENTS

SKIRT

To fit hip

32	34–36	38–40	42	44–46	in
81	86–91	96–102	107	112–117	cm

Actual size

$34^1/_2$	$37^3/_4$	41	44	$47^1/_4$	in
88	96	104	112	120	cm

Actual length

25	25	25	25	25	in
64	64	64	64	64	cm

WRAP

Actual size
$22^3/_4 \times 73^1/_4$ in
58 × 186 cm

MATERIALS

- Rowan Lurex® Shimmer in Pewter 333: 13 (14:15:16:17) × 1 oz (25 g) balls for Skirt, 22 × 1 oz (25 g) balls for Wrap
- C/2 (2.50 mm) crochet hook
- Waist length of 1 in (2.5 cm) wide elastic for Skirt

GAUGE

Motif measures $3^1/_8$ in (8 cm) along all 3 sides on C/2 hook. Change hook size if necessary to obtain this gauge.

ABBREVIATIONS

See page 15.

MOTIF

With C/2 hook, ch 4 and join with a sl st to form a ring.

Round 1: (RS) 5 ch (count as first dc and 2 ch), [1 dc into ring, 2 ch] 5 times, sl st to 3rd of 5 ch at beg of round.

Round 2: 3 ch (count as first dc), 3 dc into first ch sp, [1 dc into next dc, 3 dc into next ch sp] 5 times, sl st to top of 3 ch at beg of round. 24 sts.

Round 3: 1 ch (does NOT count as st), 1 sc into first st, *5 ch, skip 1 dc, 1 sc into next dc, 5 ch, skip 2 dc, (3 dc, 11 ch and 3 dc) into next dc, 5 ch, skip 2 dc, 1 sc into next dc, rep from * twice more, replacing sc at end of last rep with sl st to first sc.
Fasten off.

Motif is a triangle. In each corner there is an 11-ch sp, and along sides there are a further three 5-ch sps. Join motifs while working Round 3 at corners, by replacing corner (11 ch) with (5 ch, 1 sl st into corner 11-ch sp of adjacent motif, 5 ch), and at side ch sps, by replacing (5 ch) with (2 ch, 1 sl st into corresponding ch sp of adjacent motif, 2 ch).

- *The triangular motifs used here can be joined to form hexagons – so why not make a matching bag? Simply join two sets of six motifs to form two hexagons, join these hexagons and add a simple strip of crochet to form a strap.*
- *Make the skirt longer or shorter by simply adding or leaving out a band of 2 rows of motifs at the lower edge. But remember this will mean the amount of yarn you need will change!*
- *When working the waist casing of the skirt, make sure that the edge will stretch over your hips once it is sewn in place.*
- *These garments have a simple scalloped edging added afterward – but you could leave them plain or work a lacy edging if you prefer.*

SKIRT

Following diagram, make and join 198 (216: 234: 252: 270) basic motifs to form shape shown. On diagram, work the shaded section the number of times shown so that there are 11 (12: 13: 14: 15) motifs across each row. Join center back seam while joining Motifs by joining end of strip, matching A to A, B to B, C to C, etc, so that final joined Motif section forms a tube.

Hem Edging

With RS facing and using C/2 hook, rejoin yarn to lower edge at any joining point between motifs, 1 ch (does NOT count as st), work across base of each motif as follows:
*1 sc into joining point, 4 sc into next ch sp, 1 sc into each of next 3 dc, 3 sc into each of next 3 ch sps, 1 sc into each of next 3 dc, 4 sc into next ch sp, rep from * to end, sl st to first sc. 264 (288: 312: 336: 360) sts.***
Next round: (RS) 1 ch (does NOT count as st), 1 sc into st at base of 1 ch, *skip 2 sc, 6 dc into next sc, skip 2 sc, 1 sc into next sc, rep from * to end, replacing sc at end of last rep with sl st to first sc.
Fasten off.

FINISHING

Iron carefully following instructions on yarn label.

Waist Casing

Work around upper edge of Motif tube as given for Hem Edging to ***.
Next round: (RS) 3 ch (count as first dc), skip st at base of 3 ch, 1 dc into each st to end, sl st to top of 3 ch at beg of round.
Rep last round 6 times more.
Fasten off.
Fold Waist Casing in half to inside and stitch in place, leaving an opening. Thread elastic through casing and join ends. Sew casing opening closed.

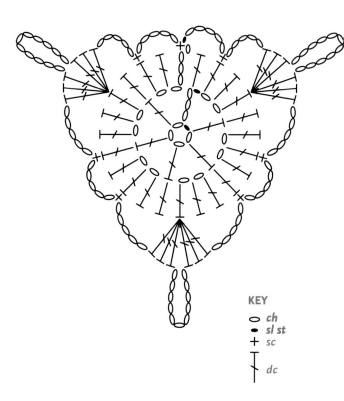

KEY
○ ch
● sl st
+ sc
┬ dc

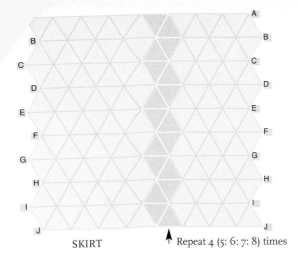

SKIRT   ↑ Repeat 4 (5: 6: 7: 8) times

WRAP

WRAP

Following diagram, make and join 360 motifs
to form shape shown. On diagram, work the
shaded section 7 times, then work unshaded
section, so that there are 22 motifs along each
long edge.

Edging

With RS facing and using C/2 hook, rejoin
yarn to one long edge at any joining point
between motifs, 1 ch (does NOT count as st),
work across edge of each motif as follows:
*1 sc into joining point, 4 sc into next ch sp,
1 sc into each of next 3 dc, 3 sc into each of next
3 ch sps, 1 sc into each of next 3 dc, 4 sc into
next ch sp, rep from * to end, sl st to first sc.
Next round: (RS) 1 ch (does NOT count as st),
1 sc into st at base of 1 ch, *skip 2 sc, 6 dc into
next sc, skip 2 sc, 1 sc into next sc, rep from *
to end, replacing sc at end of last rep with sl st
to first sc.
Fasten off.

FINISHING

Iron carefully following instructions on
yarn label.

TENDER IS THE NIGHT

Soft and gentle shades of pink, purple and gray accentuate your femininity for that special night out. Choose from the softest of pinks for an evening dress, or combine pearls and opalescent yarn for a pretty and practical bag. Use a simple, soft yarn for the little shoulder capelet, or iridescent beads for a neat little shoulder purse. Whichever design you choose, you'll look simply beautiful!

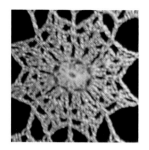

Combine simple lacy stitches and circular motifs with shimmering Lurex® and the softest of kid mohair yarns. Add a sprinkling of accent beads to create this stunning dress that will have them falling at your feet.

Evening Dress

 ADVANCED

MEASUREMENTS

To fit bust

32–34	36–38	40–42	in
81–86	91–97	102–107	cm

Actual size, at underarm

33	37$^1/_2$	41$^1/_4$	in
84	95	105	cm

Actual length, from shoulder (approx)

46	46$^1/_2$	47	in
117	118	119	cm

MATERIALS

- 40 (43: 46) × 1 oz (25 g) balls of Rowan Lurex® Shimmer in Gleam 336 (M)
- Rowan Kidsilk Haze: 3 (3: 4) × 1 oz (25 g) balls in Dewberry 600 (A – dark mauve), and 3 (4: 4) × 1 oz (25 g) balls in Grace 580 (B – pale pink)
- C/2 (2.50 mm) crochet hook
- Beads: approx 2000 (2300: 2500) × small round beads, and approx 430 (480: 540) × teardrop glass beads

GAUGE

Large motif measures 7 in (18 cm) in diameter, Small motif 3$^1/_2$ in (9 cm) in diameter, both on C/2 hook. 6 pattern repeats to 4$^1/_8$ in (10.5 cm) and 10 rows to 4 in (10 cm) measured over pattern using C/2 hook. Change hook size if necessary to obtain this gauge.

ABBREVIATIONS

dc2tog=*yo and insert hook as shown, yo and draw loop through, yo and draw through 2 loops, rep from * once more, yo and draw through all 3 loops on hook. *See also page 15.*

For how to work with beads, see pages 16–17.

LARGE MOTIF

Thread 8 round beads onto A.

With C/2 hook and A, ch 4 and join with a sl st to form a ring.

Round 1: (RS) 3 ch (count as first dc), 15 dc into ring, sl st to top of 3 ch at beg of round, turn. 16 sts.

Round 2: 1 ch (does NOT count as st), 1 beaded sc into first st, *2 ch, skip 1 dc, 1 beaded sc into next dc, rep from * to end, replacing beaded sc at end of last rep with sl st to first sc, turn. 8 ch sps.

Fasten off A and join M to first ch sp.

Round 3: 3 ch (count as first dc), (1 dc, 1 ch and 2 dc) into same ch sp, *1 ch**, (2 dc, 1 ch and 2 dc) into next ch sp, rep from * to end, ending last rep at **, sl st to top of 3 ch at beg of round. 48 sts.

Round 4: sl st across and into first ch sp, 3 ch (count as first dc), (1 dc, 1 ch and 2 dc) into same ch sp, *1 ch, 1 sc into next ch sp, 1 ch**, (2 dc, 1 ch and 2 dc) into next ch sp, rep from *

■ When working the hem flounce of this design, don't
worry that the rounds don't appear to lie flat – they
are not supposed to! They should form an undulating
wave of mohair and beaded mesh.

■ You could make this dress longer or shorter by simply
working more or less rows in the skirt section. But
remember, this will affect the amount of yarn you
need!

to end, ending last rep at **, sl st to top of 3 ch
at beg of round.

Round 5: sl st across and into first ch sp, 3 ch
(count as first dc), (1 dc, 2 ch and 2 dc) into
same ch sp, *2 ch, 1 sc into next sc, 2 ch**,
skip the next ch sp, (2 dc, 2 ch and 2 dc) into
next ch sp, rep from * to end, ending last rep
at **, sl st to top of 3 ch at beg of round.
Fasten off M. Motif is currently an 8-pointed
star shape, with a 2-ch sp at end of each point.
Thread 32 round beads onto yarn B.
Join in B to one 2-ch sp at end of one point
and cont as follows:-

Round 6: 1 ch (does NOT count as st), 1 sc into
ch sp where yarn was rejoined, *8 ch, 1 sc into
ch sp at end of next point, rep from * to end,
replacing sc at end of last rep with sl st to first
sc. 8 ch sps.

Round 7: 3 ch (count as first dc), skip sc at
base of 3 ch, *(1 dc, 1 beaded ch, [3 dc, 1 beaded
ch] 3 times and 1 dc) into next ch sp**, 1 dc
into next sc, rep from to end, ending last rep
at **, sl st to top of 3 ch at beg of round.

Round 8: 1 ch (does NOT count as st), 1 sc into
each of first 2 sts, *skip beaded ch ensuring
bead is left sitting on RS of work**, 1 sc into
each of next 3 dc, rep from * to end, ending
last rep at **, 1 sc into last dc, sl st to first sc.
96 sts.
Fasten off B.

■ The weight of the skirt section of this dress allows it to easily "drop" if left hanging up. So it is a good idea to store it flat.

■ This dress is supposed to be figure hugging and should appear a little small before it's put on. Once on the body, though, it should gently ease out to hug and flatter the figure.

Join in M to 1 sc around outer edge and cont as follows:-

Round 9: 1 ch (does NOT count as st), 1 sc into sc where yarn was rejoined, *2 ch, skip 1 sc, 1 sc into next sc, rep from * to end, replacing sc at end of last rep with sl st to first sc. 48 ch sps.

Round 10: sl st into first ch sp, 3 ch (count as first dc), (1 dc, 1 ch and 2 dc) into same ch sp, *1 ch, skip 1 ch sp**, (2 dc, 1 ch and 2 dc) into next ch sp, rep from * to end, ending last rep at **, sl st to top of 3 ch at beg of round.

Round 11: as round 4.

Round 12: sl st across and into first ch sp, 3 ch (count as first dc), (1 dc, 3 ch and 2 dc) into same ch sp, *2 ch, 1 sc into next sc, 2 ch**, (2 dc, 3 ch and 2 dc) into next ch sp, rep from * to end, ending last rep at **, sl st to top of 3 ch at beg of round.

Fasten off. Motif is a 24-pointed star shape, with a 3-ch sp at end of each point, and a sc at the base of each V between each point. Join motifs at relevant points while working round 12 by replacing (3 ch) with (1 ch, sl st into ch sp of adjacent motif, 1 ch).

SMALL MOTIF

Work as given for basic large motif to end of round 4 but using yarn B in place of yarn A.

Round 5: sl st across and into first ch sp, 3 ch (count as first dc), (1 dc, 3 ch and 2 dc) into same ch sp, *2 ch, 1 sc into next sc, 2 ch**, (2 dc, 3 ch and 2 dc) into next ch sp, rep from * to end, ending last rep at **, sl st to top of 3 ch at beg of round. Fasten off.

Motif is an 8-pointed star shape, with a 3-ch sp at end of each point, and a sc at the base of each V between each point. Join motifs at relevant points while working round 5 by replacing (3 ch) with (1 ch, sl st into ch sp of adjacent Motif, 1 ch).

UPPER MOTIF BAND

Make and join 8 (9: 10) small motifs to form a loop as follows:- leave top 2 points free, join side 2 points to side 2 points of adjacent motif, leave lower 2 points free, and join other 2 side points to next motif.

BODICE

With C/2 hook and RS facing, rejoin M to a sc between 2 free points across top of one motif of upper motif band, ***6 ch (count as 1 dc and 3 ch), working around top of upper motif band, cont as follows: *1 sc into next free point of same motif, 3 ch, 1 tr into next sc at base of V between point just worked into and point joined to next motif, 3 ch, 1 ttr into joined point of this motif and next motif, 3 ch, 1 tr into next sc at base of V between point just worked into and first free point of next motif, 3 ch, 1 sc into first free point of same motif, 3 ch**, 1 dc into sc between 2 free points across top of this motif, 3 ch rep from * to end, ending last rep at **, sl st to 3rd of 6 ch at beg of round, turn. 48 (54: 60) ch sps.

Next round: sl st across and into first ch sp, 3 ch (count as first dc), (1 dc, 2 ch and 2 dc) into same ch sp, (2 dc, 2 ch and 2 dc) into each ch sp to end, sl st to top of 3 ch at beg of round, turn. Cont in patt as follows:-

Round 1: (RS) sl st across and into first ch sp, 3 ch (count as first dc), (1 dc, 2 ch and 2 dc) into same ch sp, (2 dc, 2 ch and 2 dc) into next ch sp, rep from * to end, sl st to top of 3 ch at beg of round, turn. 48 (54: 60) patt reps. This round forms patt.****

Work in patt for a further 9 rounds, ending after a WS round.

Divide for armholes

Fasten off.

Mark points 12 (13½: 15) patt reps either side of beg/end of last round – these are underarm points. (On 2nd size, underarm point falls on a ch sp at the center of a patt rep, and on other 2 sizes, underarm point falls between 2 patt reps.) There should be 24 (27: 30) patt reps between markers – set that includes beg/end of rounds will form back, other set will form front.

Shape front

With RS facing and counting from left underarm point, skip 0 (underarm ch sp: 0) and next 3 (4: 5) ch sps, attach M to center of next ch sp and cont as follows:-

Row 1: (RS) 3 ch (count as first dc), 1 dc into same ch sp, [(2 dc, 2 ch and 2 dc) into next ch sp] 16 (16: 18) times, 2 dc into next ch sp, turn.

Row 2: 3 ch (do NOT count as st), work in patt until (2 dc, 2 ch and 1 dc) have been worked into last 2-ch sp, dc2tog working first "leg" into same ch sp as last dc and second "leg" into top of 3 ch at beg of previous row, turn.

Row 3: 3 ch (do NOT count as st), (1 dc, 1 ch and 2 dc) into first 2-ch sp, patt until one 2-ch sp remains at end of row, (2 dc and 1 ch) into last 2-ch sp, dc2tog working first "leg" into same ch sp as last dc and second "leg" into first dc of previous row, turn.

Row 4: 3 ch (count as first dc), 1 dc into first (1-ch) sp, work in patt until the one 1-ch sp remains at end of row, 1 dc into this ch sp, 1 dc into first dc of previous row, turn.

Row 5: 3 ch (count as first dc), skip last 4 dc of previous row, work in patt until (2 dc, 2 ch and 2 dc) have been worked into last 2-ch sp, skip 3 dc, 1 dc into top of 3 ch at beg of previous row, turn.

Row 6: 3 ch (count as first dc), (2 dc, 2 ch and 2 dc) into each 2-ch sp to end, 1 dc into top of 3 ch at beg of previous row. 14 (14: 16) patt reps.

Shape neck

Row 1: 3 ch (count as first dc), (2 dc, 2 ch and 2 dc) into each of first three 2-ch sps, 2 dc into next ch sp and turn, leaving rem sts unworked.

Row 2: 3 ch (do NOT count as st), skip 4 dc, (2 dc, 2 ch and 2 dc) into each of next three 2-ch sps, 1 dc into top of 3 ch at beg of previous row, turn.

Row 3: 3 ch (count as first dc), (2 dc, 2 ch and 2 dc) into each of first two 2-ch sps, (2 dc and 1 ch) into last 2-ch sp, dc2tog working first "leg" into same ch sp as last dc and second "leg" into first dc of previous row, turn.
Row 4: 3 ch (count as first dc), 1 dc into first (1-ch) sp, (2 dc, 2 ch and 2 dc) into each of next two 2-ch sps, 1 dc into top of 3 ch at beg of previous row, turn.
Row 5: 3 ch (count as first dc), (2 dc, 2 ch and 2 dc) into each of next two 2-ch sps, skip 3 dc, 1 dc into top of 3 ch at beg of previous row, turn.
Row 6: 3 ch (count as first dc), (2 dc, 2 ch and 2 dc) into each 2-ch sp to end, 1 dc into top of 3 ch at beg of previous row. 2 patt reps.
Rep row 6 until armhole measures $7^3/_4$ ($8^1/_4$: $8^1/_2$) in, 20 (21: 22) cm. Fasten off.
Return to last complete row worked before neck shaping, skip center 6 (6: 8) ch sps, attach yarn to center of next ch sp, 3 ch (count as first dc), 1 dc into same ch sp, work in patt to end. Complete second side to match first, reversing shapings.

Shape back
Return to last complete round worked before start of front shaping and, counting from right underarm point, skip 0 (underarm ch sp: 0) and next 3 (4: 5) ch sps, attach M to center of next ch sp and complete back exactly as for front. (There should be 6 (9: 10) ch sps left free at each underarm point.)

LOWER MOTIF BAND
Make and join 16 (18: 20) large motifs to form a loop as follows:- leave top 5 points free, join side 5 points to side 5 points of adjacent motif, leave lower 9 points free, and join other 5 side points to next motif.

SKIRT
With C/2 hook and RS facing, rejoin M to the sc directly below center back between 2 free points across lower edge of one motif of upper motif band and work around lower edge of motif band as for bodice from *** to ****. Work in patt for a further 5 rounds, ending after a WS round.
Next round: sl st across and into first ch sp, 3 ch (count as first dc), (1 dc, 2 ch, 2 dc, 2 ch and 2 dc) into same ch sp, *[(2 dc, 2 ch and 2 dc) into next ch sp] 5 times**, (2 dc, 2 ch, 2 dc, 2 ch and 2 dc) into next ch sp, rep from * to end, ending last rep at **, sl st to top of 3 ch at beg of round, turn.
Next round: sl st across and into first ch sp, 3 ch (count as first dc), (1 dc, 2 ch and 2 dc) into same ch sp, (2 dc, 2 ch and 2 dc) into each ch sp to end, sl st to top of 3 ch at beg of round, turn. 56 (63: 70) patt reps.
Work 8 rounds.
Next round: sl st across and into first ch sp, 3 ch (count as first dc), (1 dc, 2 ch, 2 dc, 2 ch and 2 dc) into same ch sp, *[(2 dc, 2 ch and 2 dc) into next ch sp] 6 times**, (2 dc, 2 ch, 2 dc, 2 ch and 2 dc) into next ch sp, rep from

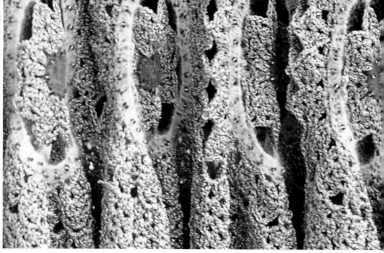

* to end, ending last rep at **sl st to top of 3 ch at beg of round, turn.

Next round: sl st across and into first ch sp, 3 ch (count as first dc), (1 dc, 2 ch and 2 dc) into same ch sp, (2 dc, 2 ch and 2 dc) into each ch sp to end, sl st to top of 3 ch at beg of round, turn. 64 (72: 80) patt reps. Work 8 rounds.

Next round: sl st across and into first ch sp, 3 ch (count as first dc), (1 dc, 2 ch, 2 dc, 2 ch and 2 dc) into same ch sp, *[(2 dc, 2 ch and 2 dc) into next ch sp] 7 times**, skip 4 dc, (2 dc, 2 ch, 2 dc, 2 ch and 2 dc) into next ch sp, rep from * to end, ending last rep at **, sl st to top of 3 ch at beg of round, turn.

Next round: sl st across and into first ch sp, 3 ch (count as first dc), (1 dc, 2 ch and 2 dc) into same ch sp, (2 dc, 2 ch and 2 dc) into each ch sp to end, sl st to top of 3 ch at beg of round, turn. 72 (81: 90) patt reps. Work 8 rounds.

Next round: sl st across and into first ch sp, 3 ch (count as first dc), (1 dc, 2 ch, 2 dc, 2 ch and 2 dc) into same ch sp, *[(2 dc, 2 ch and 2 dc) into next ch sp] 8 times**, (2 dc, 2 ch, 2 dc, 2 ch and 2 dc) into next ch sp, rep from * to end, ending last rep at **, sl st to top of 3 ch at beg of round, turn.

Next round: sl st across and into first ch sp, 3 ch (count as first dc), (1 dc, 2 ch and 2 dc) into same ch sp, (2 dc, 2 ch and 2 dc) into each ch sp to end, sl st to top of 3 ch at beg of round, turn. 80 (90: 100) patt reps.

Work 8 rounds.

Join skirt to lower motif band

Next round: sl st across and into first ch sp, 1 ch (does NOT count as st), 1 sc into same ch sp, 3 ch, 1 sc into center free point of one motif around upper edge of lower motif band, *3 ch, 1 sc into next ch sp of skirt, 4 ch, 1 sc into next free point of same motif, 4 ch, 1 sc into next ch sp of skirt, 5 ch, 1 sc into next free point of same motif, 5 ch, 1 sc into next ch sp of skirt, 5 ch, 1 sc into first free point of next motif, 5 ch, 1 sc into next ch sp of skirt, 4 ch, 1 sc into next free point of same motif, 4 ch**, 1 sc into next ch sp of skirt, 3 ch, 1 sc into next (center) free point of same motif, rep from * to end, ending last rep at **, sl st to first sc. Fasten off.

SKIRT HEM FLOUNCE

With C/2 hook and RS facing, rejoin M to ch sp of first free point of any motif around lower edge of lower motif mand and work around lower edge of lower motif band as follows:
1 ch (does NOT count as st), 1 sc into same free point as where yarn was joined, *3 ch, 1 dc into next sc at base of V after point just worked into, 3 ch, 1 sc into next free point (or 1 dc in to pair of joined points), rep from * to end, replacing sc at end of last rep with sl st to first sc, turn. 320 (360: 400) ch sps.

Round 1: (WS) sl st across and into first ch sp, 3 ch (count as first dc), (1 dc, 2 ch and 2 dc)

into same ch sp, (2 dc, 2 ch and 2 dc) into each ch sp to end, sl st to top of 3 ch at beg of round, turn. 320 (360: 400) patt reps. Work in patt for a further 8 rounds.
Thread 320 (360: 400) teardrop beads onto B. Join in yarn B to first ch sp.

Round 10: (RS) using B, 3 ch (count as first dc), (1 dc, 2 ch and 2 dc) into same ch sp, *1 beaded ch**, (2 dc, 2 ch and 2 dc) into next ch sp, rep from * to end, ending last rep at **, sl st to top of 3 ch at beg of round, turn.

Round 11: Using M, 1 ch (does NOT count as st), 1 sc into last ch sp of previous round placing this sc so that it sits after bead, *3 ch, 1 sc into next 2-ch sp, 3 ch**, (1 sc, 3 ch and 1 sc) into next beaded ch sp ensuring bead sits between the 2 sc, rep from * to end, ending last rep at **, 1 sc into next beaded ch sp placing this sc before the beaded ch, 2 ch, 1 sc into first sc, turn.

Round 12: Using M, 1 ch (does NOT count as st), 1 sc into ch sp partly formed by 2 ch at end of previous round, *3 ch, 1 sc into next ch sp, rep from * until sc has been worked into last 3-ch sp, 2 ch, 1 sc into first sc, turn. Break off M.

Rounds 13 and 14: Using B, as round 12. Join in A.

Rounds 15 and 16: Using A, as round 12.

Round 17: Using B, as round 12. Break off B.

Thread 960 (1080: 1200) round beads onto A.

Round 18: Using A, 1 ch (does NOT count as st), 1 sc into ch sp partly formed by 2 ch at end of previous round, *1 ch, 1 beaded ch, 1 ch, 1 sc into next ch sp, rep from * to end, replacing sc at end of last rep with sl st to first sc. Fasten off.

FINISHING

Iron very carefully following instructions on yarn label, taking care not to damage beads. Join shoulder seams.

Armhole edgings (both alike)

With RS facing and using C/2 hook, rejoin M at underarm point, 1 ch (does NOT count as st), work one round of sc evenly around entire armhole edge, ending with sl st to first sc, turn.

Round 1: (WS) 1 ch (does NOT count as st), 1 sc into each sc to end, sl st to first sc. Fasten off.

Neck edging and flounce

With RS facing and using C/2 hook, rejoin M at one shoulder seam, 1 ch (does NOT count as st), work one round of sc evenly around entire neck edge, ensuring there are an even number of sc and ending with sl st to first sc, turn.
Set this ball of yarn aside to complete neck edging.
Thread teardrop beads onto B.
Join in B and work flounce as follows:-

Round 1: (WS) Working into back loops only of previous round (those nearest RS of work) and using B, 3 ch (count as first dc), (1 dc, 2 ch and

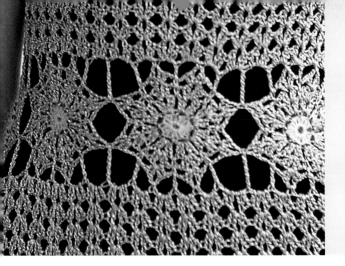

2 dc) into first sc, *skip 1 sc, (2 dc, 2 ch and 2 dc) into next sc, rep from * to last sc, skip last sc, sl st to top of 3 ch at beg of round, turn.

Round 2: Using B, sl st across and into first ch sp, 3 ch (count as first dc), (1 dc, 2 ch and 2 dc) into same ch sp, *1 beaded ch**, (2 dc, 2 ch and 2 dc) into next ch sp, rep from * to end, ending last rep at **, sl st to top of 3 ch at beg of round, turn.

Join in second ball of M.

Round 3: Using M, 1 ch (does NOT count as st), 1 sc into last ch sp of previous round placing this sc so that it sits after bead, *3 ch, 1 sc into next 2-ch sp, 3 ch**, (1 sc, 3 ch and 1 sc) into next beaded ch sp ensuring bead sits between the 2 sc, rep from * to end, ending last rep at **, 1 sc into next beaded ch sp placing this sc before the beaded ch, 2 ch, 1 sc into first sc, turn.

Round 4: Using M, 1 ch (does NOT count as st), 1 sc into ch sp partly formed by 2 ch at end of previous round, *3 ch, 1 sc into next ch sp, rep from * until sc has been worked into last 3-ch sp, 2 ch, 1 sc into first sc, turn.
Break off M.

Rounds 5 and 6: Using B, as round 4.
Join in A.

Rounds 7 and 8: Using A, as round 4.
Break off A.

Rounds 9 and 10: Using B, as round 4.
Thread round beads onto B.

Round 11: Using B, 1 ch (does NOT count as st), 1 sc into ch sp partly formed by 2 ch at end

of previous round, *1 ch, 1 beaded ch, 1 ch, 1 sc into next ch sp, rep from * to end, replacing sc at end of last rep with sl st to first sc.
Fasten off.

Pick up ball of M left at end of first round of edging and flounce and, with WS facing, complete neck edging as follows:- 1 ch (does NOT count as st), working into rem free loop of sc already used for flounce and into both loops of each sc between those used for flounce (so leaving flounce sitting on RS of work) work 1 sc into each sc to end, sl st to first sc.
Fasten off.

Keep your shoulders warm in this chevron stitch capelet. The soft yarn combines a glittering golden thread with the cuddliest of yarns to add just a dash of sparkle.

Capelet

 EASY

MEASUREMENTS

One size, to fit bust
34–42 in
86–107 cm

Actual width at lower edge
58³/₄ in
149.5 cm

Actual length
17¹/₄ in
44 cm

MATERIALS
- 6 × 1³/₄ oz (50 g) balls of RYC Soft Lux in Basalt 005
- H/8 (5.00 mm) crochet hook

GAUGE
Based on a double crochet fabric gauge of 14¹/₂ sts and 7¹/₂ rows to 4 in (10 cm) using H/8 hook. Change hook size if necessary to obtain this gauge.

ABBREVIATIONS
See page 15.

Neck border and ties
With H/8 hook, ch 168.
Row 1: (RS) 1 sc into 2nd ch from hook, 1 sc into each ch to end, turn. 167 sts.
Row 2: 1 ch (does NOT count as st), 1 sc into each sc to end.
Fasten off.
These 2 rows complete Neck Border and Ties.

Main section
With RS facing, skip first 44 sc of Row 2, rejoin yarn to next sc and cont as follows:-
Row 1: (RS) 3 ch (count as first dc), 1 dc into sc at base of 3 ch, *1 dc into each of next 2 sc, skip 1 sc, 1 dc into each of next 2 sc, (1 dc, 2 ch and 1 dc) into next sc, rep from * 11 times more, 1 dc into each of next 2 sc, skip 1 sc, 1 dc into each of next 2 sc, 2 dc into next sc and turn, leaving rem 44 sc unworked. 104 sts, 13 patt reps in total.
Row 2: 3 ch (count as first dc), 1 dc into dc at base of 3 ch, *1 dc into each of next 2 dc, skip 2 dc, 1 dc into each of next 2 dc**, (1 dc, 2 ch and 1 dc) into next ch sp, rep from * to end, ending last rep at **, 2 dc into top of 3 ch at beg of previous row, turn.
Row 3: 3 ch (count as first dc), 2 dc into dc at base of 3 ch, *1 dc into each of next 2 dc, skip 2 dc, 1 dc into each of next 2 dc**, (2 dc, 2 ch

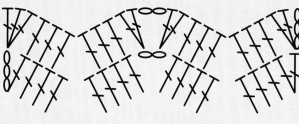

and 2 dc) into next ch sp, rep from * to end, ending last rep at **, 3 dc into top of 3 ch at beg of previous row, turn. 130 sts.

Row 4: 3 ch (count as first dc), 1 dc into dc at base of 3 ch, *1 dc into each of next 3 dc, skip 2 dc, 1 dc into each of next 3 dc**, (1 dc, 2 ch and 1 dc) into next ch sp, rep from * to end, ending last rep at **, 2 dc into top of 3 ch at beg of previous row, turn.

Row 5: 3 ch (count as first dc), 2 dc into dc at base of 3 ch, *1 dc into each of next 3 dc, skip 2 dc, 1 dc into each of next 3 dc**, (2 dc, 2 ch and 2 dc) into next ch sp, rep from * to end, ending last rep at **, 3 dc into top of 3 ch at beg of previous row, turn. 156 sts.

Rows 6 and 7: 3 ch (count as first dc), 1 dc into dc at base of 3 ch, *1 dc into each of next 4 dc, skip 2 dc, 1 dc into each of next 4 dc**, (1 dc, 2 ch and 1 dc) into next ch sp, rep from * to end, ending last rep at **, 2 dc into top of 3 ch at beg of previous row, turn.

Row 8: 3 ch (count as first dc), 2 dc into dc at base of 3 ch, *1 dc into each of next 4 dc, skip 2 dc, 1 dc into each of next 4 dc**, (2 dc, 2 ch and 2 dc) into next ch sp, rep from * to end, ending last rep at **, 3 dc into top of 3 ch at beg of previous row, turn. 182 sts.

Rows 9 to 11: 3 ch (count as first dc), 1 dc into dc at base of 3 ch, *1 dc into each of next 5 dc,

- ■ Made from a really soft, extra fine merino wool, angora and nylon mix – with just a touch of shimmering glitz – this capelet is the perfect way to keep warm and look elegant!
- ■ As this capelet is worked in mainly double crochet and uses quite a thick yarn, you'll be amazed at just how quickly it will grow.
- ■ Worked from the neck downward, you could easily carry on and work a few more rows if you wanted a longer length.
- ■ Because this capelet is made in one piece, there are no seams to sew up afterward. Just crochet it and go!

skip 2 dc, 1 dc into each of next 5 dc**, (1 dc, 2 ch and 1 dc) into next ch sp, rep from * to end, ending last rep at **, 2 dc into top of 3 ch at beg of previous row, turn.

Row 12: 3 ch (count as first dc), 2 dc into dc at base of 3 ch, *1 dc into each of next 5 dc, skip 2 dc, 1 dc into each of next 5 dc**, (2 dc, 2 ch and 2 dc) into next ch sp, rep from * to end, ending last rep at **, 3 dc into top of 3 ch at beg of previous row, turn. 208 sts.

Rows 13 to 16: 3 ch (count as first dc), 1 dc into dc at base of 3 ch, *1 dc into each of next 6 dc, skip 2 dc, 1 dc into each of next 6 dc**, (1 dc, 2 ch and 1 dc) into next ch sp, rep from * to end, ending last rep at **, 2 dc into top of 3 ch at beg of previous row, turn.

Row 17: 3 ch (count as first dc), 2 dc into dc at base of 3 ch, *1 dc into each of next 6 dc, skip 2 dc, 1 dc into each of next 6 dc**, (2 dc, 2 ch and 2 dc) into next ch sp, rep from * to end, ending last rep at **, 3 dc into top of 3 ch at beg of previous row, turn. 234 sts.

Rows 18 to 22: 3 ch (count as first dc), 1 dc into dc at base of 3 ch, *1 dc into each of next 7 dc, skip 2 dc, 1 dc into each of next 7 dc**, (1 dc, 2 ch and 1 dc) into next ch sp, rep from * to end, ending last rep at **, 2 dc into top of 3 ch at beg of previous row, turn.

Row 23: 3 ch (count as first dc), 2 dc into dc at base of 3 ch, *1 dc into each of next 7 dc, skip 2 dc, 1 dc into each of next 7 dc**, (2 dc, 2 ch and 2 dc) into next ch sp, rep from * to end, ending last rep at **, 3 dc into top of 3 ch at beg of previous row, turn. 260 sts.

Rows 24 to 33: 3 ch (count as first dc), 1 dc into dc at base of 3 ch, *1 dc into each of next 8 dc, skip 2 dc, 1 dc into each of next 8 dc**, (1 dc, 2 ch and 1 dc) into next ch sp, rep from * to end, ending last rep at **, 2 dc into top of 3 ch at beg of previous row, turn.

Turning work again so that RS of work is facing, work 1 row of crab st (sc worked from left to right, instead of right to left) along top of last row, working into each dc and ch of previous row.
Fasten off.

FINISHING

Iron carefully, following instructions on yarn label.

Made in a stunning eyelash yarn that combines classic cream with opalescent shimmer, this little shrug ensures you look stylish and stay cozy and warm.

Shrug

MEASUREMENTS

To fit bust

32–34	36–38	40–42	in
81–86	91–97	102–107	cm

Actual size, measured from cuff to cuff

52	56	58^1/$_4$	in
132	142	148	cm

Actual width of section worked in rows

15^3/$_4$	16^1/$_2$	17^1/$_4$	in
40	42	44	cm

MATERIALS

- 9 (9: 11) × 1^3/$_4$ oz (50 g) balls of Lion Brand Fun Fur in Ivory 098
- K/10^1/$_2$ (7.00 mm) crochet hook

GAUGE

9 sts and 7 rows to 10 cm (4 in) measured over pattern using K/10^1/$_2$ hook. Change hook size if necessary to obtain this gauge.

ABBREVIATIONS

dc2tog – *yo and insert hook as indicated, yo and draw loop through, yo and draw through 2 loops, rep from * once more, yo and draw through all 3 loops on hook.

See also page 15.

Shrug is worked in one piece from cuff to cuff

With K/10^1/$_2$ hook, ch 20 (22: 22) and join with a sl st to form a ring.

Round 1: (RS) 3 ch (count as first dc), skip first ch, 1 dc into each ch to end, sl st to top of 3 ch at beg of round, turn. 20 (22: 22) sts. Cont in patt as follows:

Round 2: (WS) sl st between 3 ch at beg and dc at end of previous round, 3 ch (count as first dc), 1 dc between last 2 dc of previous round, *1 dc between next 2 dc, rep from * until dc has been worked between 3 ch and dc at beg of previous round, sl st to top of 3 ch at beg of round, turn. This round forms patt – dcs worked between dcs of previous round. Cont in patt for a further 2 rounds.

Round 5: sl st between 3 ch at beg and dc at end of previous round, 3 ch (count as first dc), 1 dc into same place as sl st – 1 st increased, 1 dc between last dc of previous round and next dc, *1 dc between next 2 dc, rep from * until dc has been worked between 3 ch and dc at beg of previous round, 1 dc into same place as last dc – 1 st increased, sl st to top of 3 ch at beg of round, turn. 22 (24: 24) sts.

Working all increases as set by last round, inc 1 st at each end of every 3rd round until there are 36 (38: 40) sts.

Work 4 (6: 3) rounds – 30 (32: 32) rounds completed. Work should measure 17 (18: 18) in, 43 (46: 46) cm.

Now work patt in rows, not rounds, as follows:

Next row: 3 ch (count as first dc), 1 dc between last 2 dc of previous row, *1 dc between next 2 dc, rep from * until dc has been worked between 3 ch and dc at beg of previous row, turn.

This row forms patt worked in rows.

Work a further 30 (33: 37) rows.

Next row: 3 ch (count as first dc), 1 dc between last 2 dc of previous row, *1 dc between next 2 dc, rep from * until dc has been worked between 3 ch and dc at beg of previous row, sl st to top of 3 ch at beg of round, turn.

Work should measure 18 (19¹/₂: 22) in, 46 (50: 56) cm, along row-end edges.

Now working patt in rounds as before, not rows, cont as follows:

Work 4 (6: 3) rounds.

Next round: sl st between 3 ch at beg and dc at end of previous round, 3 ch (do NOT count as st), 1 dc between last dc of previous round and next dc – 1 st decreased, *1 dc between next 2 dc, rep from * until dc has been worked

KEY

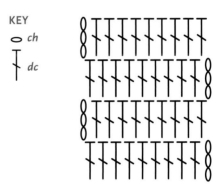

o — ch

⊤ — dc

between first 2 dc of previous round, dc2tog working first "leg" between next 2 dc and 2nd "leg" between 3 ch and dc at beg of previous round – 1 st decreased, sl st to top of 3 ch at beg of round, turn. 34 (36: 38) sts.

Working all decreases as set by last round, dec 1 st at each end of every 3rd round until 20 (22: 22) sts rem.

Work a further 4 rounds.

Fasten off.

FINISHING

Do NOT iron.

This simple belt is made up of a row of bead-encrusted flower motifs, worked in a casual cotton yarn. Vary the length of the belt by adding more or working fewer motifs to make the size that fits you best.

Flower Motif Belt

 EASY

MEASUREMENTS
Actual size
2³/₄ × 61¹/₂ in
7 × 156 cm

MATERIALS
- 1 × 1³/₄ oz (50 g) ball of Rowan Cotton Glace in each of color A (magenta 818), color B (purple 815), and color C (black 727)
- Faceted beads: 96 in each of 2 colors for Star Motifs, and 88 in 3rd color for Joining Motifs
- C/2 (2.50 mm) crochet hook

GAUGE
Star Motif measures 2³/₄ in (7 cm) in diameter (excluding beads) on C/2 hook. Change hook size if necessary to obtain this gauge.

ABBREVIATIONS
See page 15.

For how to work with beads, see pages 16–17.

STAR MOTIF
Thread 16 beads onto yarn A – 8 of one color for outer edge and 8 of second color for center.
With C/2 hook and yarn A, ch 4 and join with a sl st to form a ring.

Round 1: (RS) 1 ch (does NOT count as st), [1 sc into ring, 1 beaded ch – make sure bead is left sitting on RS of work] 8 times, sl st to first sc.
Round 2: 7 ch (count as first dc and 4 ch), skip sc at base of 7 ch and next beaded ch, *1 dc into next sc, 4 ch, skip 1 beaded ch, rep from * to end, sl st to 3rd of 7 ch at beg of round. 8 ch sps.
Round 3: 1 ch (does NOT count as st), (1 sc, 1 hdc, 1 dc, 1 tr, 1 beaded ch, 1 tr, 1 dc, 1 hdc and 1 sc) into each ch sp to end, sl st to first sc. Fasten off.
Motif is an 8-pointed star shape with a bead sitting at the end of each point.
Make a further 11 motifs in this way, making another 5 using yarn A and 6 using yarn B.

JOINING MOTIF
Star motifs are joined to these motifs as round 3 is worked.
Thread 8 beads onto yarn C.
With C/2 hook and yarn C, ch 6 and join with a sl st to form a ring.
Round 1: (RS) 1 ch (does NOT count as st), 16 sc into ring, sl st to first sc.
Round 2: 1 ch (does NOT count as st), 1 sc into sc at base of 1 ch, 1 sc into next sc, *(1 sc, 8 ch and 1 sc) into next sc**, 1 sc into each of next 3 sc, rep from * to end, ending last rep at **, 1 sc into next sc, sl st to first sc.

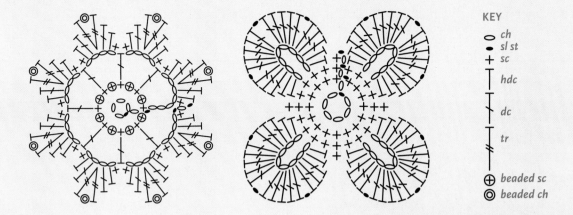

Round 3: 1 ch (does NOT count as st), 1 sc into sc at base of 1 ch, *skip 2 sc, (2 hdc, 3 dc, 1 beaded ch, 5 dc, 1 beaded ch and 5 dc) into next ch sp, 1 sl st into beaded ch at end of one point of a star motif worked in yarn A, (3 dc and 2 hdc) into same ch sp, skip 2 sc, 1 sc into next sc, skip 2 sc, (2 hdc and 3 dc) into next ch sp, 1 sl st into beaded ch at end of next point of same star motif worked in yarn A, (5 dc, 1 beaded ch, 5 dc, 1 beaded ch, 3 dc and 2 hdc) into same ch sp, skip 2 sc, 1 sc into next sc, skip 2 sc, (2 hdc, 3 dc, 1 beaded ch, 5 dc, 1 beaded ch and 5 dc) into next ch sp, 1 sl st into beaded ch at end of one point of a star motif worked in yarn B, (3 dc and 2 hdc) into same ch sp, skip 2 sc, 1 sc into next sc, skip 2 sc, (2 hdc and 3 dc) into next ch sp, 1 sl st into beaded ch at end of next point of same star motif worked in yarn B, (5 dc, 1 beaded ch, 5 dc, 1 beaded ch, 3 dc and 2 hdc) into same ch sp, skip 2 sc, sl st to first sc. Fasten off. Make a further 10 joining motifs in this way, joining them to form one long strip of 23 alternating star and joining motifs, using alternating colors of star motifs and ensuring there are 2 points of each star motif left free between those joined to joining motifs.

FINISHING

Iron following instructions on yarn label.

Totally covered in iridescent beads, this pouch-style bag is made all in one piece so there's no sewing up afterward! It's worked in rounds of beaded chain and single crochet using a fine Lurex® yarn.

Beaded Evening Bag

 ADVANCED

MEASUREMENTS

Actual size, excluding tassel
6³/₄ × 7¹/₂ in
17 × 19 cm

MATERIALS

- 3 × 1 oz (25 g) balls of Rowan Lurex® Shimmer in Black 334
- C/2 (2.50 mm) crochet hook
- Approx 2,900 beads

GAUGE

24 sts and 27 rows to 4 in (10 cm) measured over beaded pattern using C/2 hook. Change hook size if necessary to obtain this gauge.

ABBREVIATIONS

sc2tog - *insert hook as indicated, yo and draw loop through, rep from * once more, yo and draw through all 3 loops on hook. *See also page 15. For how to work with beads, see pages 16–17.*

MAIN SECTION

Thread beads onto yarn. With C/2 hook, ch 8, sl st in first ch to form a ring.

Foundation round: (WS) 1 ch (does NOT count as st), 2 sc into each ch to end, sl st to first sc, turn. 16 sts.

Cont in beaded patt as follows:

Round 1: (RS) 1 ch (does NOT count as st), 1 sc into each of first 2 sc, [1 beaded ch, 1 sc into each of next 2 sc] 3 times, [1 sc into each of next 2 sc, 1 beaded ch] 3 times, 1 sc into each of last 2 sc, sl st to first sc, turn. (NOTE: While working the patt, the beaded ch do NOT count as sts. When working across top of foll rounds, skip the beaded ch and only work into the sc of previous rounds. Ensure all beads sit on RS of work by gently easing them through to that side of the work.)

Round 2: 1 ch (does NOT count as st), 2 sc into first sc, [1 beaded ch, 1 sc into each of next 2 sc] 3 times, 1 beaded ch, 2 sc into each of next 2 sc, [1 beaded ch, 1 sc into each of next 2 sc] 3 times, 1 beaded ch, 2 sc into last sc, sl st to first sc, turn. 20 sts.

Round 3: 1 ch (does NOT count as st), 2 sc into first sc, [1 beaded ch, 1 sc into each of next 2 sc] 4 times, 1 beaded ch, 2 sc into each of next 2 sc, [1 beaded ch, 1 sc into each of next 2 sc] 4 times, 1 beaded ch, 2 sc into last sc, sl st to first sc, turn. 24 sts.

Round 4: 1 ch (does NOT count as st), 2 sc into first sc, [1 beaded ch, 1 sc into each of next 2 sc] 5 times, 1 beaded ch, 2 sc into each of next 2 sc, [1 beaded ch, 1 sc into each of next 2 sc] 5 times, 1 beaded ch, 2 sc into last sc, sl st to first sc, turn. 28 sts.

■ *If you want to line the bag, simply cut lining fabric to the size of the finished bag, adding seam allowance. Join the seams, place the lining inside and slip stitch the lining in place around the opening edges.*

■ *Make sure you leave the yarn holding the beads of the base tassel quite loose so that the beads can move around a little.*

Round 5: 1 ch (does NOT count as st), 2 sc into first sc, [1 beaded ch, 1 sc into each of next 2 sc] 6 times, 1 beaded ch, 2 sc into each of next 2 sc, [1 beaded ch, 1 sc into each of next 2 sc] 6 times, 1 beaded ch, 2 sc into last sc, sl st to first sc, turn. 32 sts.

Cont in this way, increasing 4 sts on every round, until the foll round has been worked:

Round 13: 1 ch (does NOT count as st), 2 sc into first sc, [1 beaded ch, 1 sc into each of next 2 sc] 14 times, 1 beaded ch, 2 sc into each of next 2 sc, [1 beaded ch, 1 sc into each of next 2 sc] 14 times, 1 beaded ch, 2 sc into last sc, sl st to first sc, turn. 64 sts.

Round 14: 1 ch (does NOT count as st), 1 sc into first sc, [1 beaded ch, 1 sc into each of next 2 sc] 31 times, 1 beaded ch, 1 sc into last sc, sl st to first sc, turn.

Round 15: 1 ch (does NOT count as st), 2 sc into first sc, 1 sc into next sc, [1 beaded ch, 1 sc into each of next 2 sc] 14 times, 1 beaded ch, 1 sc into next sc, 2 sc into each of next 2 sc, 1 sc into next sc, [1 beaded ch, 1 sc into each of next 2 sc] 14 times, 1 beaded ch, 1 sc into next sc, 2 sc into last sc, sl st to first sc, turn. 68 sts.

Round 16: 1 ch (does NOT count as st), 1 sc into each of first 2 sc, [1 beaded ch, 1 sc into each of next 2 sc] 16 times, 1 sc into each of next 2 sc, [1 beaded ch, 1 sc into each of next 2 sc] 16 times, sl st to first sc, turn.

Round 17: 1 ch (does NOT count as st), 2 sc into first sc, [1 beaded ch, 1 sc into each of next 2 sc] 16 times, 1 beaded ch, 2 sc into each of next 2 sc, [1 beaded ch, 1 sc into each of next 2 sc] 16 times, 1 beaded ch, 2 sc into last sc, sl st to first sc, turn. 72 sts.

Round 18: 1 ch (does NOT count as st), 1 sc into first sc, [1 beaded ch, 1 sc into each of next 2 sc] 35 times, 1 beaded ch, 1 sc into last sc, sl st to first sc, turn.

Round 19: 1 ch (does NOT count as st), 2 sc into first sc, 1 sc into next sc, [1 beaded ch, 1 sc into each of next 2 sc] 16 times, 1 beaded ch, 1 sc into next sc, 2 sc into each of next 2 sc, 1 sc into next sc, [1 beaded ch, 1 sc into each of next 2 sc] 16 times, 1 beaded ch, 1 sc into next sc, 2 sc into last sc, sl st to first sc, turn. 76 sts.

Round 20: 1 ch (does NOT count as st), 1 sc into each of first 2 sc, [1 beaded ch, 1 sc into each of next 2 sc] 18 times, 1 sc into each of next 2 sc, [1 beaded ch, 1 sc into each of next 2 sc] 18 times, sl st to first sc, turn.

Round 21: 1 ch (does NOT count as st), 1 sc into first sc, [1 beaded ch, 1 sc into each of next 2 sc] 37 times, 1 beaded ch, 1 sc into last sc, sl st to first sc, turn.

Round 22: As round 20.

Round 23: 1 ch (does NOT count as st), 2 sc into first sc, [1 beaded ch, 1 sc into each of next 2 sc] 18 times, 1 beaded ch, 2 sc into each of next 2 sc, [1 beaded ch, 1 sc into each of next 2 sc] 18 times, 1 beaded ch, 2 sc into last sc, sl st to first sc, turn. 80 sts.

Round 24: 1 ch (does NOT count as st), 1 sc

```
+◎+  +◎+  +◎+  +◎+  +◎+  +◎+
 +   +◎+  +◎+  +◎+  +◎+  +◎+   +
+◎+  +◎+  +◎+  +◎+  +◎+  +◎+
 +   +◎+  +◎+  +◎+  +◎+  +◎+   +
+◎+  +◎+  +◎+  +◎+  +◎+  +◎+
```

into first sc, [1 beaded ch, 1 sc into each of next 2 sc] 39 times, 1 beaded ch, 1 sc into last sc, sl st to first sc, turn.

Round 25: 1 ch (does NOT count as st), 1 sc into each of first 2 sc, [1 beaded ch, 1 sc into each of next 2 sc] 19 times, 1 sc into each of next 2 sc, [1 beaded ch, 1 sc into each of next 2 sc] 19 times, sl st to first sc, turn.

Rounds 26 to 29: As rounds 24 and 25, twice.

Round 30: As round 24.

Round 31: 1 ch (does NOT count as st), sc2tog over first 2 sc, [1 beaded ch, 1 sc into each of next 2 sc] 18 times, 1 beaded ch, [sc2tog over next 2 sc] twice, [1 beaded ch, 1 sc into each of next 2 sc] 18 times, 1 beaded ch, sc2tog over last 2 sc, sl st to first sc2tog, turn. 76 sts.

Rounds 32 and 33: As rounds 20 and 21.

Round 34: As round 20.

Round 35: 1 ch (does NOT count as st), sc2tog over first 2 sc, 1 sc into next sc, [1 beaded ch, 1 sc into each of next 2 sc] 16 times, 1 beaded ch, 1 sc into next sc, [sc2tog over next 2 sc] twice, 1 sc into next sc, [1 beaded ch, 1 sc into each of next 2 sc] 16 times, 1 beaded ch, 1 sc into next sc, sc2tog over last 2 sc, sl st to first sc2tog, turn. 72 sts.

Round 36: As round 18.

Round 37: 1 ch (does NOT count as st), 1 sc into each of first 2 sc, [1 beaded ch, 1 sc into each of next 2 sc] 17 times, 1 sc into each of next 2 sc, [1 beaded ch, 1 sc into each of next 2 sc] 17 times, sl st to first sc, turn.

Round 38: As round 18.

Round 39: 1 ch (does NOT count as st), sc2tog over first 2 sc, [1 beaded ch, 1 sc into each of next 2 sc] 16 times, 1 beaded ch, [sc2tog over next 2 sc] twice, [1 beaded ch, 1 sc into each of next 2 sc] 16 times, 1 beaded ch, sc2tog over last 2 sc, sl st to first sc, turn. 68 sts.

Round 40: As round 16.

Round 41: 1 ch (does NOT count as st), 1 sc into first sc, [1 beaded ch, 1 sc into each of next 2 sc] 33 times, 1 beaded ch, 1 sc into last sc, sl st to first sc, turn.

Round 42: As round 16.

Round 43: 1 ch (does NOT count as st), sc2tog over first 2 sc, 1 sc into next sc, [1 beaded ch, 1 sc into each of next 2 sc] 14 times, 1 beaded ch, 1 sc into next sc, [sc2tog over next 2 sc] twice, 1 sc into next sc, [1 beaded ch, 1 sc into each of next 2 sc] 14 times, 1 beaded ch, 1 sc into next sc, sc2tog over last 2 sc, sl st to first sc2tog, turn. 64 sts.

Round 44: As round 14.

Round 45: 1 ch (does NOT count as st), 1 sc into each of first 2 sc, [1 beaded ch, 1 sc into each of next 2 sc] 15 times, 1 sc into each of next 2 sc, [1 beaded ch, 1 sc into each of next 2 sc] 15 times, sl st to first sc, turn.

Round 46: As round 14.

Round 47: 1 ch (does NOT count as st), sc2tog over first 2 sc, [1 beaded ch, 1 sc into each of next 2 sc] 14 times, 1 beaded ch, [sc2tog over next 2 sc] twice, [1 beaded ch, 1 sc into each of next 2 sc] 14 times, 1 beaded ch, sc2tog over last 2 sc, sl st to first sc2tog, turn. 60 sts.

- This bag uses beads with an oil-on-water finish to them but you could make a brighter, funky version by using a selection of different colored beads. Mix them all together before you start threading them onto the yarn and thread them so that the colors appear randomly.
- The bag is quite heavy as there are so many beads – so make sure you attach the strap securely!

Round 48: 1 ch (does NOT count as st), 1 sc into each of first 2 sc, [1 beaded ch, 1 sc into each of next 2 sc] 14 times, 1 sc into each of next 2 sc, [1 beaded ch, 1 sc into each of next 2 sc] 14 times, sl st to first sc, turn.

Round 49: 1 ch (does NOT count as st), 1 sc into first sc, [1 beaded ch, 1 sc into each of next 2 sc] 29 times, 1 beaded ch, 1 sc into last sc, sl st to first sc, turn.

Round 50: As round 48.

Shape flap

Row 51: (RS) 1 ch (does NOT count as st), 1 sc into first sc, [1 beaded ch, 1 sc into each of next 2 sc] 14 times, 1 beaded ch, 1 sc into next sc, turn.

Work in rows on this set of 30 sts only for flap.

Row 52: 1 ch (does NOT count as st), 1 sc into each of first 2 sc, [1 beaded ch, 1 sc into each of next 2 sc] 14 times, turn.

Row 53: 1 ch (does NOT count as st), 1 sc into first sc, [1 beaded ch, 1 sc into each of next 2 sc] 14 times, 1 beaded ch, 1 sc into last sc, turn.

Rows 54 and 55: As rows 52 and 53.

Row 56: As row 52.

Row 57: 1 ch (does NOT count as st), sc2tog over first 2 sc, 1 sc into next sc, [1 beaded ch, 1 sc into each of next 2 sc] 12 times, 1 beaded ch, 1 sc into next sc, sc2tog over last 2 sc, turn. 28 sts.

Row 58: 1 ch (does NOT count as st), 1 sc into first sc, [1 beaded ch, 1 sc into each of next 2 sc] 13 times, 1 beaded ch, 1 sc into last sc, turn.

Row 59: 1 ch (does NOT count as st), sc2tog over first 2 sc, [1 beaded ch, 1 sc into each of next 2 sc] 12 times, 1 beaded ch, sc2tog over last 2 sc, turn. 26 sts.

Row 60: 1 ch (does NOT count as st), 1 sc into each of first 2 sc, [1 beaded ch, 1 sc into each of next 2 sc] 12 times, turn.

Row 61: 1 ch (does NOT count as st), sc2tog over first 2 sc, 1 sc into next sc, [1 beaded ch, 1 sc into each of next 2 sc] 10 times, 1 beaded ch, 1 sc into next sc, sc2tog over last 2 sc, turn. 24 sts.

Row 62: 1 ch (does NOT count as st), 1 sc into first sc, [1 beaded ch, 1 sc into each of next 2 sc] 11 times, 1 beaded ch, 1 sc into last sc, turn.

Row 63: 1 ch (does NOT count as st), sc2tog over first 2 sc, [1 beaded ch, 1 sc into each of next 2 sc] 10 times, 1 beaded ch, sc2tog over last 2 sc, turn. 22 sts.

Row 64: 1 ch (does NOT count as st), sc2tog over first 2 sc, [1 beaded ch, 1 sc into each of next 2 sc] 9 times, 1 beaded ch, sc2tog over last 2 sc, turn. 20 sts.

Row 65: 1 ch (does NOT count as st), sc2tog over first 2 sc, [1 beaded ch, 1 sc into each of next 2 sc] 8 times, 1 beaded ch, sc2tog over last 2 sc, turn. 18 sts.

Row 66: 1 ch (does NOT count as st), sc2tog over first 2 sc, [1 beaded ch, 1 sc into each of next 2 sc] 7 times, 1 beaded ch, sc2tog over last 2 sc, turn. 16 sts.

Row 67: 1 ch (does NOT count as st), sc2tog over first 2 sc, [1 beaded ch, 1 sc into each of

next 2 sc] 6 times, 1 beaded ch, sc2tog over last 2 sc, turn. 14 sts.

Row 68: 1 ch (does NOT count as st), sc2tog over first 2 sc, [1 beaded ch, 1 sc into each of next 2 sc] 5 times, 1 beaded ch, sc2tog over last 2 sc, turn. 12 sts.

Row 69: 1 ch (does NOT count as st), sc2tog over first 2 sc, [1 beaded ch, 1 sc into each of next 2 sc] 4 times, 1 beaded ch, sc2tog over last 2 sc, turn. 10 sts.

Row 70: 1 ch (does NOT count as st), sc2tog over first 2 sc, [1 beaded ch, 1 sc into each of next 2 sc] 3 times, 1 beaded ch, sc2tog over last 2 sc, turn. 8 sts.

Row 71: 1 ch (does NOT count as st), sc2tog over first 2 sc, [1 beaded ch, 1 sc into each of next 2 sc] twice, 1 beaded ch, sc2tog over last 2 sc, turn. 6 sts.

Row 72: 1 ch (does NOT count as st), sc2tog over first 2 sc, 1 beaded ch, 1 sc into each of next 2 sc, 1 beaded ch, sc2tog over last 2 sc, turn. 4 sts.

Row 73: 1 ch (does NOT count as st), sc2tog over first 2 sc, sc2tog over last 2 sc. 2 sts. Fasten off.

FLAP AND OPENING EDGING

With C/2 hook and RS facing, attach yarn to Main Section on first sc after turning point for flap, 1 ch (does NOT count as st), 1 sc into sc where yarn was rejoined, 1 sc into each of next 29 sc of round 50, then work in sc evenly around outer shaped edge of flap, ending with sl st to first sc, turn.

Next round: (WS) 1 ch (does NOT count as st), 1 beaded sc into each sc to end, sl st to first sc. Fasten off.

BASE TASSEL

With C/2 hook and **WS** facing, attach yarn to foundation ch edge of main section, 1 ch (does NOT count as st), 1 beaded sc into each of 8 foundation ch, sl st to first sc, do NOT turn.

Next round: (WS) 1 ch (does NOT count as st), 1 beaded sc into each beaded sc to end, sl st to first sc, do NOT turn.

Rep last round twice more.

Work fringe

Next round: Slide 40–50 beads up next to sl st closing last round and work a sl st into first st of last round leaving beads to form a loop, *slide another 40–50 beads by next to last sl st and work a sl st into next st leaving beads to form a loop, rep from * 6 times more. Fasten off.

STRAP

With C/2 hook, ch 201.

Row 1: (RS) 1 beaded sc into 2nd ch from hook, 1 beaded sc into each ch to end, turn.

Row 2: 1 ch (does NOT count as st), 1 sc into first beaded sc, 1 sc into each beaded sc to end, turn.

Row 3: 1 ch (does NOT count as st), 1 beaded sc into each sc to end. Fasten off.

Attach ends of strap inside upper edge of main section as in photograph.

Combine accent shades of pink and purple Lurex® yarns with twinkling beads to make this stunning flower. Complete with leaves and twirling tendrils, it's sure to jazz up any outfit.

CORSAGE

 INTERMEDIATE

MEASUREMENTS

Actual size, excluding streamers
5¹/₂ × 7¹/₂ in
14 × 19 cm

MATERIALS

- 4 × E316 (pink), 3 × E155 (lilac), 4 × E3837 (purple), 2 × E699 (green) of 8.7–yd balls of DMC Light Effects Needlepoint Thread
- C/2 (2.50 mm) crochet hook
- Approx 210 clear, 50 pink, 230 green, and 80 purple beads
- Brooch back

GAUGE

Flower Center measures 2 in (5 cm) in diameter using C/2 hook. Change hook size if necessary to obtain this gauge.

ABBREVIATIONS

sc2tog=*insert hook as indicated, yo and draw loop through, rep from * once more,
yo and draw through all 3 loops on hook;
sc3tog=*insert hook as indicated, yo and draw loop through, rep from *twice more,
yo and draw through all 4 loops on hook.
See also page 15.

For how to work with beads, see pages 16–17.

FLOWER CENTER

Thread 96 assorted pink and clear beads onto pink yarn.
With C/2 hook and pink, ch 4 and join with a sl st to form a ring.
Round 1: (RS) 1 ch (does NOT count as st), 8 sc into ring, sl st to first sc. 8 sts.
Round 2: 1 ch (does NOT count as st), 3 sc into each sc to end, sl st to first sc. 24 sts.
Round 3: 3 ch (count as first dc), 3 dc into sc at base of 3 ch, 4 dc into each sc to end, sl st to top of 3 ch at beg of round. 96 sts.
Round 4: 1 ch (does NOT count as st), 1 sc into first st, *1 ch, 1 beaded ch, 1 ch, 1 sc into next dc, rep from * to end, replacing sc at end of last rep with sl st to first sc.
Fasten off.

SMALL PETALS

Thread 85 clear beads onto lilac yarn.
With C/2 hook and lilac, ch 4 and join with a sl st to form a ring.
Round 1: (RS) 1 ch (does NOT count as st), 10 sc into ring, sl st to first sc. 10 sts.
Round 2: 6 ch (count as first dc and 3 ch), skip sc at base of 6 ch and next sc, [1 dc into next sc, 3 ch, skip 1 sc] 4 times, sl st to 3rd of 6 ch at beg of round. 5 ch sps.

Work petals

Row 1: (RS) sl st into first ch sp, 1 ch (does NOT count as st), 5 sc into same ch sp, turn.

Row 2: 1 ch (does NOT count as st), 2 sc into each of first 2 sc, 1 sc into next sc, 2 sc into each of last 2 sc, turn. 9 sts.

Row 3: 1 ch (does NOT count as st), 2 sc into first sc, 1 sc into each of next 7 sc, 2 sc into last sc, turn. 11 sts.

Row 4: 1 ch (does NOT count as st), 2 sc into first sc, 1 sc into next sc, 1 beaded sc into next sc, 1 sc into each of next 7 sc, 2 sc into last sc, turn. 13 sts.

Row 5: 1 ch (does NOT count as st), 2 sc into first sc, 1 sc into each of next 11 sc, 2 sc into last sc, turn. 15 sts.

Row 6: 1 ch (does NOT count as st), 2 sc into first sc, 1 sc into each of next 9 sc, 1 beaded sc into next sc, 1 sc into each of next 3 sc, 2 sc into last sc, turn. 17 sts.

Row 7: 1 ch (does NOT count as st), 1 sc into each sc to end, turn.

Row 8: 1 ch (does NOT count as st), 1 sc into each of first 3 sc, 1 beaded sc into next sc, 1 sc into each of next 2 sc, 1 beaded sc into next sc, 1 sc into each of last 10 sc, turn.

Row 9: As row 7.

Row 10: 1 ch (does NOT count as st), 1 sc into first sc, sc2tog over next 2 sc, 1 sc into each of next 7 sc, 1 beaded sc into next sc, 1 sc into each of next 3 sc, sc2tog over next 2 sc, 1 sc into last sc, turn. 15 sts.

Row 11: 1 ch (does NOT count as st), 1 sc into first sc, [sc2tog over next 2 sts] twice, 1 sc into each of next 5 sc, [sc2tog over next 2 sts] twice, 1 sc into last sc, turn. 11 sts.

Row 12: 1 ch (does NOT count as st), 1 sc into first sc, [sc2tog over next 2 sts] twice, 1 beaded sc into next sc, [sc2tog over next 2 sts] twice, 1 sc into last sc, turn. 7 sts.

Row 13: 1 ch (does NOT count as st), 1 sc into first sc, sc2tog over next 2 sts, 1 sc into next sc, sc2tog over next 2 sts, 1 sc into last sc, turn. 5 sts.

Row 14: 1 ch (does NOT count as st), 1 sc into first sc, sc3tog over next 3 sts, 1 sc into last sc, turn. 3 sts.

Row 15: 1 ch (does NOT count as st), sc3tog over all 3 sts and fasten off.

These 15 rows complete one petal.

*With RS facing, rejoin yarn with a sl st into next ch sp of round 2, 1 ch (does NOT count as st), 5 sc into this ch sp, turn.

Now work rows 2 to 15 again.

Rep from * until 5 petals have been completed.

Work edging

With WS facing, rejoin yarn with a sl st into a dc of round 2 between petals, 1 ch (does NOT count as st), work one round of sc evenly around outer edges of all petals, working into each dc of round 2 between petals, placing a bead on every 3rd sc and ending with sl st to first sc. Fasten off. Lay flower center onto center of small petals and sew in place as in photograph.

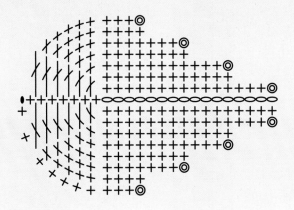

Leaf pattern

LARGE PETALS

Thread 150 assorted purple and clear beads onto purple yarn.

With C/2 hook and purple, ch 4 and join with a sl st to form a ring.

Round 1: (RS) 1 ch (does NOT count as st), 9 sc into ring, sl st to first sc. 9 sts.

Round 2: 3 ch (count as first dc), 1 dc into base of 3 ch, 2 dc into each sc to end, sl st to top of 3 ch at beg of round. 18 sts.

Round 3: 6 ch (count as first dc and 3 ch), skip st at base of 6 ch and next dc, [1 dc into next dc, 3 ch, skip 1 dc] 8 times, sl st to 3rd of 6 ch at beg of round. 9 ch sps.

Now complete as given for Small Petals from start of working petals – there will be a total of 9 petals.

Lay flower center and small petals onto center of large petals and sew in place as in photograph.

STREAMERS

Thread 200 green beads onto green yarn.

With C/2 hook and green, ch 31, 1 beaded sc into 2nd ch from hook, 1 beaded sc into each of next 29 ch, 51 ch, 1 beaded sc into 2nd ch from hook, 1 beaded sc into each of next 49 ch, 41 ch, 1 beaded sc into 2nd ch from hook, 1 beaded sc into each of next 39 ch, 46 ch, 1 beaded sc into 2nd ch from hook, 1 beaded sc into each of next 44 ch, 36 ch, 1 beaded sc into 2nd ch from hook, 1 beaded sc into each of next 34 ch.

Fasten off.

Sew streamers in place to back of large petals as in photograph.

LEAVES (make 3)

Thread 8 green beads onto green yarn.

With C/2 hook and green, ch 16.

Row 1: (RS) 1 beaded ch, 1 sc into 3rd ch from hook, 1 sc into each of next 13 ch, 3 sc into last ch, now working back along other side of foundation ch, 1 sc into each of next 15 ch, turn.

Row 2: 1 beaded ch, skip first sc, 1 sc into each sc to last 3 sc, working 3 sc into central sc at base of leaf, turn.

Rows 3 to 7: As row 2.

Row 8: 1 beaded ch, skip first sc, 1 sc into each sc to central sc at base of Leaf, 1 sl st into same sc as last sc.

Fasten off.

Sew leaves to back of large petals as in photograph. Attach brooch back.

Completely encrusted with pearl teardrop beads, this bag will shimmer all night long! It's made in simple rounds of plain and beaded single crochet so there's very little sewing up to do afterward.

Pearl Evening Bag

 ADVANCED

MEASUREMENTS

Actual size, approx
$12^3/_4 \times 7^3/_4$ in
32.5 × 20 cm

MATERIALS

- 8 × $1^3/_4$ oz (50 g) balls of Lion Brand Glitterspun in Silver 150
- C/2 (2.50 mm) crochet hook
- Approx 2,500 pearl teardrop beads
- Firm card 12 in × 6 in (30 cm × 15 cm)
- Piece of lining fabric 12 in × 12 in (30 cm × 30 cm)
- 14 in (40 cm) of $1^3/_4$ in (3 cm) wide firm petersham ribbon
- One large press stud fastener

GAUGE

28 sts and 32 rows to 10 cm (4 in) measured over beaded double crochet fabric using 2.50 mm hook. Change hook size if necessary to obtain this gauge.

ABBREVIATIONS

sc2tog - *insert hook as indicated, yo and draw loop through, rep from * once more, yo and draw through all 3 loops on hook.
See also page 15.
For how to work with beads, see pages 16–17.

MAIN SECTION

With C/2 hook, ch 42.

Round 1: (RS) 2 sc into 2nd ch from hook, 1 sc into each of next 39 ch, 4 sc into last ch, working back along other side of foundation ch work 1 sc into each of next 39 ch, 2 sc into last ch – this is same ch as used for 2 sc at beg of round, sl st to first sc, turn. 86 sts.

Round 2: 1 ch (does NOT count as st), 2 sc into each of first 2 sc, 1 sc into each of next 39 sc, 2 sc into each of next 4 sc, 1 sc into each of next 39 sc, 2 sc into each of last 2 sc, sl st to first sc, turn. 94 sts.

Round 3: 1 ch (does NOT count as st), 1 sc into each sc to end, sl st to first sc, turn.

Round 4: 1 ch (does NOT count as st), *[1 sc into next sc, 2 sc into next sc] twice, 1 sc into each of next 39 sc, [1 sc into next sc, 2 sc into next sc] twice, rep from * once more, sl st to first sc, turn. 102 sts.

Round 5: 1 ch (does NOT count as st), *[1 sc into each of next 2 sc, 2 sc into next sc] twice, 1 sc into each of next 39 sc, [1 sc into each of next 2 sc, 2 sc into next sc] twice, rep from * once more, sl st to first sc, turn. 110 sts.

Round 6: As round 3.

Round 7: 1 ch (does NOT count as st), *[1 sc into each of next 3 sc, 2 sc into next sc] twice, 1 sc into each of next 39 sc, [1 sc into each of

■ The pearl beads are only placed on wrong side rounds so, to avoid sliding them along the yarn, try working from two skeins of yarn at the same time. Thread the beads onto one skein and use this for the beaded rounds, using a plain skein for the other rounds.

next 3 sc, 2 sc into next sc] twice, rep from * once more, sl st to first sc, turn. 118 sts.

Round 8: 1 ch (does NOT count as st), *[1 sc into each of next 4 sc, 2 sc into next sc] twice, 1 sc into each of next 39 sc, [1 sc into each of next 4 sc, 2 sc into next sc] twice, rep from * once more, sl st to first sc, turn. 126 sts.

Round 9: As round 3.

Round 10: 1 ch (does NOT count as st), *[1 sc into each of next 5 sc, 2 sc into next sc] twice, 1 sc into each of next 39 sc, [1 sc into each of next 5 sc, 2 sc into next sc] twice, rep from * once more, sl st to first sc, turn. 134 sts.

Round 11: 1 ch (does NOT count as st), *[1 sc into each of next 6 sc, 2 sc into next sc] twice, 1 sc into each of next 39 sc, [1 sc into each of next 6 sc, 2 sc into next sc] twice, rep from * once more, sl st to first sc, turn. 142 sts.

Round 12: As round 3.

Round 13: 1 ch (does NOT count as st), *[1 sc into each of next 7 sc, 2 sc into next sc] twice, 1 sc into each of next 39 sc, [1 sc into each of next 7 sc, 2 sc into next sc] twice, rep from * once more, sl st to first sc, turn. 150 sts.

Round 14: 1 ch (does NOT count as st), *[1 sc into each of next 8 sc, 2 sc into next sc] twice, 1 sc into each of next 39 sc, [1 sc into each of next 8 sc, 2 sc into next sc] twice, rep from * once more, sl st to first sc, turn. 158 sts.

Round 15: As round 3.

Round 16: 1 ch (does NOT count as st), *[1 sc into each of next 9 sc, 2 sc into next sc] twice, 1 sc into each of next 39 sc, [1 sc into each of next 9 sc, 2 sc into next sc] twice, rep from *

once more, sl st to first sc, turn. 166 sts.

Round 17: 1 ch (does NOT count as st), *[1 sc into each of next 10 sc, 2 sc into next sc] twice, 1 sc into each of next 39 sc, [1 sc into each of next 10 sc, 2 sc into next sc] twice, rep from * once more, sl st to first sc, turn. 174 sts.

Round 18: As round 3.

Round 19: 1 ch (does NOT count as st), *[1 sc into each of next 5 sc, 2 sc into next sc, 1 sc into each of next 6 sc] twice, 1 sc into each of next 39 sc, [1 sc into each of next 5 sc, 2 sc into next sc, 1 sc into each of next 6 sc] twice, rep from * once more, sl st to first sc, turn. 182 sts.

Round 20: As round 3.

These 20 rounds complete base. Trace around shape of base and cut out this shape from firm card.

Round 21: 1 ch (does NOT count as st), working into back loops only of sts of previous row, 1 sc into each sc to end, sl st to first sc, **turn.**

Cont in beaded sc fabric as follows:

Round 1: (WS) 1 ch (does NOT count as st), *1 sc into next sc, 1 beaded sc into next sc, rep from * to end, sl st to first sc, turn.

Round 2: 1 ch (does NOT count as st), 1 sc into each sc to end, sl st to first sc, turn.

Round 3: 1 ch (does NOT count as st), *1 beaded sc into next sc, 1 sc into next sc, rep from * to end, sl st to first sc, turn.

Round 4: As round 2.

These 4 rounds form beaded sc fabric.

Work in beaded sc fabric for a further 50 rounds, ending with a RS row.

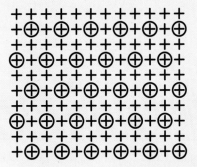

KEY

+ sc

⊕ beaded ch

Shape top band

Next round: (WS) 1 ch (does NOT count as st), *1 sc into next sc, [sc2tog over next 2 sc] 3 times, rep from * to end, sl st to first sc, turn. 104 sts.

Next round: 1 ch (does NOT count as st), 1 sc into each sc to end, sl st to first sc, turn.

Rep last round 17 times more.

Fasten off.

HANDLE

With C/2 hook, ch 14 and join with a sl st to form a ring.

Round 1: (RS) 1 ch (does NOT count as st), 1 sc into each sc to end. 14 sts.

Round 2: 1 sc into each sc to end.

Rep round 2 until Handle is 21¼ in (54 cm) long.

Fasten off.

FINISHING

Do NOT iron.

Join ends of petersham ribbon, overlapping them by 1 in (2.5 cm). Fold last 9 rounds of top band to inside and stitch in place, slipping loop of petersham ribbon underneath. Attach ends of handle inside top band as in photograph. Cover card base shape with lining fabric, then insert base into bag and slip stitch in place. Attach stud fastener to close upper edge.

This simple slip of a dress, worked in a combination of double crochet and a lacy mesh stitch, uses a silky yarn and has silver teardrop beads around the hem to add extra interest.

Slip Dress

INTERMEDIATE

MEASUREMENTS

To fit bust

32	34	36	38	40	42	in
81	86	91	97	102	107	cm

Actual size, at underarm

32	33³/₄	35³/₄	37³/₄	39³/₄	41³/₄	in
81	86	91	96	101	106	cm

Actual length, from shoulder (approx)

37	37¹/₂	37³/₄	38	38¹/₂	39	in
94	95	96	97	98	99	cm

MATERIALS

- 16 (18: 20: 22: 24: 25) × 1³/₄ oz (50 g) balls of Crystal Palace Crème in black 2020 (wool/silk blend)
- B/1 (2.00 mm) crochet hook
- 310 (334: 350: 374: 390: 414) × silver teardrop pearl beads

GAUGE

32 sts and 15 rows to 4 in (10 cm) measured over treble fabric using B/1 hook. 4 pattern repeats to 4¹/₄ in (11 cm) and 16 rows to 4 in (10 cm) measured over mesh pattern using B/1 hook. Change hook size if necessary to obtain this gauge.

ABBREVIATIONS

sc2tog – *insert hook as indicated, yo and draw loop through, rep from * once more, yo and draw through all 3 loops on hook;

dc2tog – *yo and insert hook as indicated, yo and draw loop through, yo and draw through 2 loops, rep from * once more, yo and draw through all 3 loops on hook; **dc3tog** – *yo and insert hook as indicated, yo and draw loop through, yo and draw through 2 loops, rep from * twice more, yo and draw through all 4 loops on hook.

See also page 15.

For how to work with beads, see pages 16–17.

BODICE

With B/1 hook, ch 260 (276: 292: 308: 324: 340) and join with a sl st to form a ring.

Foundation round: (RS) 3 ch (count as first dc), skip ch at base of 3 ch, 1 dc into each ch to end, sl st to top of 3 ch at beg of round, turn. 260 (276: 292: 308: 324: 340) sts.

Cont in dc fabric as follows:

Round 1: (WS) 3 ch (count as 1 dc), skip st at base of 3 ch, 1 dc into each dc to end, sl st to top of 3 ch at beg of round, turn.

This round forms dc fabric. (Beg and end of

■ Twilleys Silky is a very slippery yarn and the stitches can easily fall undone. Each time you put your work down, it's a good idea to slip the working loop onto a safety pin to make sure it does not unravel!

■ You could make this dress longer or shorter by simply working more or less rows in the skirt section. But remember this will mean the amount of yarn you need will change!

■ As the dress will "drop" slightly in wear, it's a good idea to measure the length of the skirt section with it hanging, not laid flat.

■ Be sure to thread the tie through the underbust casing before working the second tassel end as the beads will be difficult to thread through the crochet.

■ Teardrop pearl beads come in two types – those that have their threading hole across the top narrow end, and those that are drilled from top to bottom. Make sure you buy the kind with the hole at the top!

rounds is center back point.)
Work a further 10 rounds in dc fabric, ending with a WS round.
Fasten off.

Shape top edge

Skip first 73 (79: 85: 91: 97: 103) sts of next round, rejoin yarn to next dc with RS facing, 3 ch (count as first dc), skip dc where yarn was rejoined, 1 dc into each of next 52 (54: 56: 58: 60: 62) dc, dc3tog over next 3 dc, 1 dc into next dc (this is dc before center front point) and turn, leaving rem sts unworked.
Work in dc fabric in **rows** on this set of 55 (57: 59: 61: 63: 65) sts only for first side of top edge.
Next row: 3 ch (count as first dc), dc3tog over next 3 sts – 2 sts decreased, 1 dc into each dc to last 4 sts, dc3tog over next 3 sts – 2 sts decreased, 1 dc into top of 3 ch at beg of previous row, turn. 51 (53: 55: 57: 59: 61) sts.
Working all decreases as set by last row, dec 2 sts at each end of next 8 (10: 6: 8: 4: 6) rows, ending with a WS row. 19 (13: 31: 25: 43: 37) sts.
Next row: (RS) 3 ch (count as first dc), dc2tog over next 2 sts – 1 st decreased, 1 dc into each dc to last 4 sts, dc3tog over next 3 sts – 2 sts decreased, 1 dc into top of 3 ch at beg of previous row, turn.
Next row: 3 ch (count as first dc), dc3tog over next 3 sts – 2 sts decreased, 1 dc into each dc to last 3 sts, dc2tog over next 2 sts – 1 st decreased, 1 dc into top of 3 ch at beg of previous row, turn. 13 (7: 25: 19: 37: 31) sts.

Rep last 2 rows 1 (0: 3: 2: 5: 4) times more, then first of these rows again. 4 sts.
Next row: (WS) 3 ch (do NOT count as st), dc3tog over last 3 sts.
Fasten off.
Return to last complete round worked, with RS facing rejoin yarn to next dc after first side of top edge, 3 ch (count as first dc), skip dc where yarn was rejoined, dc3tog over next 3 dc, 1 dc into each of next 53 (55: 57: 59: 61: 63) dc and turn, leaving rem sts unworked. 55 (57: 59: 61: 63: 65) sts.
Working all shaping as set by first side, dec 2 sts at center front edge of next 14 (14: 16: 16: 18: 18) rows and at the same time dec 2 sts at side edge of next 9 (11: 7: 9: 5: 7) rows, then 1 st at this edge on foll 5 (3: 9: 7: 13: 11) rows. 4 sts.
Next row: (WS) 3 ch (do NOT count as st), dc3tog over last 3 sts.
Fasten off.

SKIRT

With RS facing and using B/1 hook, rejoin yarn to foundation ch edge of bodice at center back, 1 ch (does NOT count as st), 1 sc into each foundation ch, sl st to first sc, turn. 260 (276: 292: 308: 324: 340) sts.
Round 2: (WS) 1 ch (does NOT count as st), 1 sc into each sc to end, sl st to first sc, turn.
Round 3: 4 ch (count as first dc and 1 ch), skip sc at base of 4 ch and next sc, *1 dc into next sc, 1 ch, skip 1 sc, rep from * to end, sl st to 3rd of 4 ch at beg of round, turn.

KEY

o   *ch*
+   *sc*
T   *dc*

Round 4: 1 ch (does NOT count as st), 1 sc into each ch sp and dc to end, sl st to first sc, turn.

Round 5: As round 2.

These 5 rounds complete underbust section.

Next round: (WS) 1 ch (does NOT count as st), 1 sc into first sc, [5 ch, skip 3 sc, 1 sc into next sc] 8 (7: 8: 8: 9: 8) times, [5 ch, skip 2 sc, 1 sc into next sc] 22 (26: 26: 30: 30: 34) times, [5 ch, skip 3 sc, 1 sc into next sc] 16 (16: 18: 16: 18: 18) times, [5 ch, skip 2 sc, 1 sc into next sc] 22 (26: 26: 30: 30: 34) times, [5 ch, skip 3 sc, 1 sc into next sc] 7 (6: 7: 7: 8: 7) times, 5 ch, skip 3 sc, sl st to sc at beg of round, turn.

76 (82: 86: 92: 96: 102) ch sps.

Cont in mesh patt as follows:

Round 1: (RS) 3 ch (count as first dc), 2 dc into sc at base of 3 ch, *1 sc into next ch sp, 5 ch, skip 1 sc, 1 sc into next ch sp**, 5 dc into next sc, rep from * to end, ending last rep at **, 2 dc into same place as dc at beg of round, sl st to top of 3 ch at beg of round. 38 (41: 43: 46: 48: 51) patt reps.

Round 2: 1 ch (does NOT count as st), 1 sc into same place as sl st at end of previous round, *5 ch, skip (2 dc and 1 sc), 1 sc into next ch sp**, 5 ch, skip (1 sc and 2 dc), 1 sc into next dc, rep from * to end, ending last rep at **, 2 ch, skip (1 sc and 2 dc), 1 dc into sc at beg of round.

Round 3: 1 ch (does NOT count as st), 1 sc into ch sp partly formed by dc at end of previous round, *5 ch, skip 1 sc, 1 sc into next ch sp, 5 dc into next sc, 1 sc into next ch sp, rep from * to end, replacing sc at end of last rep with sl st to first sc.

Round 4: sl st across and into center of first ch sp, 1 ch (does NOT count as st), 1 sc into same ch sp, *5 ch, skip (1 sc and 2 dc), 1 sc into next dc, 5 ch, skip (2 dc and 1 sc), 1 sc into next ch sp, rep from * to end, replacing sc at end of last rep with sl st to first sc.

These 4 rounds form mesh patt.

Cont in mesh patt until Skirt measures 24½ (24¾: 24¾: 25: 25: 25½) ins, 62 (63: 63: 64: 64: 65) cm, from round 5 of underbust section, ending with patt round 2 or 4. 76 (82: 86: 92: 96: 102) ch sps. Fasten off.

Work hem border

Thread beads onto yarn.

With RS facing, rejoin yarn into one ch sp at center back and cont as follows:

Round 1: 1 ch (does NOT count as st), 1 sc into ch sp where yarn was rejoined, *7 ch, (1 sc, 1 beaded ch and 1 sc) into next ch sp, rep from * to end, replacing sc at end of last rep with sl st to first sc.

Round 2: sl st along and into center of first ch sp, 1 ch (does NOT count as st), 1 sc into same ch sp, *9 ch, (1 sc, 1 beaded ch and 1 sc) into next ch sp, rep from * to end, replacing sc at end of last rep with sl st to first sc.

Round 3: sl st along and into center of first ch sp, 1 ch (does NOT count as st), 1 sc into same ch sp, *6 ch, 1 beaded ch, skip beaded ch, sl st to next ch, 5 ch, (1 sc, 1 beaded ch and 1 sc) into next ch sp, rep from * to end, replacing sc at end of last rep with sl st to first sc.

Fasten off.

FINISHING

Do NOT iron.

Front neck edging

With RS facing and using B/1 hook, rejoin yarn at fasten-off point at top of left front edge, 1 ch (does NOT count as st), work one row of sc evenly down left front slope, then up right front slope to other fasten-off point, turn.

Next row: (WS) 1 ch (does NOT count as st), 1 sc into each sc to end, working sc2tog at either side of base of center front V neck, turn.

Rep last row once more.

Do NOT fasten off.

Armhole and back edging and shoulder straps

With RS facing and using B/1 hook, attach separate length of yarn to beg of last row of front neck edging, ch 94 (94: 96: 96: 98: 98) (for left shoulder strap) and fasten off.

With RS facing, using B/1 hook and yarn left at end of front neck edging, ch 95 (95: 97: 97: 99: 99) (for right shoulder strap), 1 sc into 2nd ch from hook, 1 sc into each of next 93 (93: 95: 95: 97: 97) ch, work one row of sc evenly down right armhole edge, across back, then up left armhole edge to ch at top of front neck edging, 1 sc into each ch to end, turn.

Next row: (WS) 1 ch (does NOT count as st), 1 sc into each sc to end, skipping sc as required to ensure edging lies flat, turn.

Rep last row once more. Fasten off.

Underbust tie

Threads 6 beads onto yarn.

Using B/1 hook, make a ch approx 55 (57, 5, 61, 63, 66) in, 140 (145: 150: 155: 160: 165) cm long and cont as follows: 22 ch, 1 beaded ch, skip beaded ch, 1 sc into each of next 22 ch, 1 sl st into next ch, 29 ch, 1 beaded ch, skip beaded ch, 1 sc into each of next 29 ch, 1 sl st into same ch as already worked into for first strand of tassel, 16 ch, 1 beaded ch, skip beaded ch,

1 sc into each of next 16 ch, 1 sl st into is same ch as already worked into for first and second strands of tassel, 1 sc into each ch to end, break off yarn leaving a very long end but do NOT fasten off. Leave working loop on a safety pin.

Starting and ending at center front, thread tie in and out of round 3 of underbust section. Insert hook into working loop and complete tassel at other end of tie as follows: 22 ch, 1 beaded ch, skip beaded ch, 1 sc into each of next 22 ch, 1 sl st into is same ch as last sc was worked into before tie was threaded through, 29 ch, 1 beaded ch, skip beaded ch, 1 sc into each of next 29 ch, 1 sl st into same ch as already worked into for first strand of tassel, 16 ch, 1 beaded ch, skip beaded ch, 1 sc into each of next 16 ch, 1 sl st into is same ch as already worked into for first and second strands of tassel.

Fasten off.

Try on dress and adjust length of shoulder straps, attaching them to inside of back edging.

Index

Suppliers and useful addresses

Berroco, Inc.
Elmdale Rd.
Uxbridge, MA 01569
Tel: (508) 278-2527

Classic Elite Yarns, Inc.
122 Western Avenue
Lowell, MA 01851
Tel: (978) 453-2837
www.classiceliteyarns.com

Coats & Clark
Consumer Services
P.O. Box 12229
Greeneville, SC 29612-0224
Tel: (800) 648-1479
www.coatsandclark.com

Crystal Palace Yarns
160 23rd Street
Richmond, CA 94804
Tel: (510) 237-9988
www.crystalpalaceyarns.com

DMC Creative World
77 South Hackensack Avenue
Building 10F
South Kearny, NJ 07032
Tel: (973) 589-0606
www.dmc-usa.com

Lion Brand Yarn Co.
34 West 15th St.
New York, NY 10011
Tel: (212) 243-8995

Red Heart® Yarns
Two Lakepointe Plaza
4135 So. Stream Blvd.
Charlotte, NC 28217
www.coatsandclark.com

Caron International
P.O. Box 222
Washington, NC 27889
www.caron.com

Michael's Stores, Inc.
8000 Bent Branch Drive
Irving, TX 75063
Tel: (800) 642-4235
www.michaels.com